AUSC

compiled and edited by
Teresa Świebocka

English edition prepared by
Jonathan Webber
and Connie Wilsack

hwitz

A History
in Photographs

THE AUSCHWITZ–BIRKENAU
STATE MUSEUM
Oświęcim

INDIANA UNIVERSITY PRESS
Bloomington and Indianapolis

KSIĄŻKA I WIEDZA
Warsaw

First published in Polish in 1990 by the Państwowe Muzeum Oświęcim–Brzezinka (Auschwitz–Birkenau State Museum) and Książka i Wiedza under the title *Auschwitz: Zbrodnia przeciwko ludzkości* (Auschwitz: Crime against humanity).

Library of Congress Cataloging-in-Publication Data
Auschwitz. English.
  Auschwitz: a history in photographs /
compiled and edited by Teresa Świebocka: English
edition prepared by Jonathan Webber and Connie
Wilsack.
    p.   cm.
  Includes bibliographical references.
  ISBN 0-253-35581-8
  1. Auschwitz (Poland: Concentration camp)—Pictorial
works. 2. Holocaust, Jewish (1939–1945)—Pictorial
works. I. Świebocka, Teresa. II. Webber, Jonathan. III.
Wilsack, Connie.
D805.P7A8813   1993
940.53'174386—dc20   93-1083

1 2 3 4 5 97 96 95 94 93

KiW ISBN 83-05-12643-9

Typeset in Times by 'Print', Warsaw
Printed and bound by TIZ Zrinski, Čakovec, Croatia

Contents

Preface to the English Edition

THROUGH more than 280 documentary photographs from the archives of the Auschwitz–Birkenau State Museum and reproductions of artistic works by former prisoners, this book records the history of Auschwitz and what it looks like today. It includes photographs taken by the Nazis of the construction and expansion of the camp, of individual prisoners and scenes from daily life, and of the machinery of mass murder itself—the gas chambers and crematoria; clandestine photographs, taken by prisoners; aerial photographs, taken by the Allies; photographs taken at the time of the liberation of the camp by Soviet forces; and photographs of the site as it is today. The captions accompanying the photographs give the contemporary reader a clear grasp of the historical facts. Supplementary extracts from documentary sources give an insight into the perspective both of the victims and of the Nazis. Finally, a series of essays place the photographs in context; an afterword, 'Personal Reflections on Auschwitz Today', offers some thoughts on how one may attempt to comprehend today the significance and implications of the appalling horrors that Auschwitz has come to symbolize.

This book first appeared in Polish in 1990. In preparing it for presentation to an English-speaking readership we have revised the texts of the essays, added the afterword, and expanded the captions to the historical photographs. The intention throughout has been to present the subject as fully as possible in the light of current historical understanding and in a manner that is accessible to readers who may have no first-hand knowledge of the subject. It should be emphasized, however, that the history of Auschwitz is often complicated on specific minor points, as circumstances and procedures changed frequently. Hence the reader will occasionally find references to 'sometimes' or 'often', in order to avoid tedious detailed exposition of minor variations in Nazi policy or practice which can be found fully documented elsewhere in the very extensive literature on Auschwitz and the Holocaust. We have therefore chosen to keep bibliographic references to such literature to a minimum, and to focus instead on the research undertaken by the staff of the Auschwitz–Birkenau State Museum based on the primary sources in the Museum's archives.

Care has been taken throughout to use terminology that is sensitive to the subject-matter. For example, the term 'extermination', although frequently used in the context of Auschwitz and the Holocaust more generally, is not really an appropriate way of referring to the mass murder of human beings. For the same reason we have referred to the five main installations of mass murder in Auschwitz as 'gas chambers and crematoria', whereas the Nazis, presumably for reasons of euphemism, had called these buildings simply 'crematoria'; certainly the phrase 'gas ovens', which may often be found in the literature, is not correct.

The way in which the term 'Auschwitz' has been used also needs some explanation. We have used this name for the Auschwitz camp system as a whole and also to refer to Auschwitz in the symbolic sense, as a concept or idea. To distinguish between the three principal camps at Auschwitz we have referred to 'Auschwitz I', 'Auschwitz II-Birkenau', and 'Auschwitz III-Monowitz'. The town that the Germans called Auschwitz is referred to by its Polish name, Oświęcim.

This book is dedicated to all those who suffered in Auschwitz—those who died, and those who survived—men and women, children and infants, from many countries and many nations, the overwhelming majority of them Jews.

T.Ś., J.W., and C.W.

Oświęcim and Oxford
February 1993

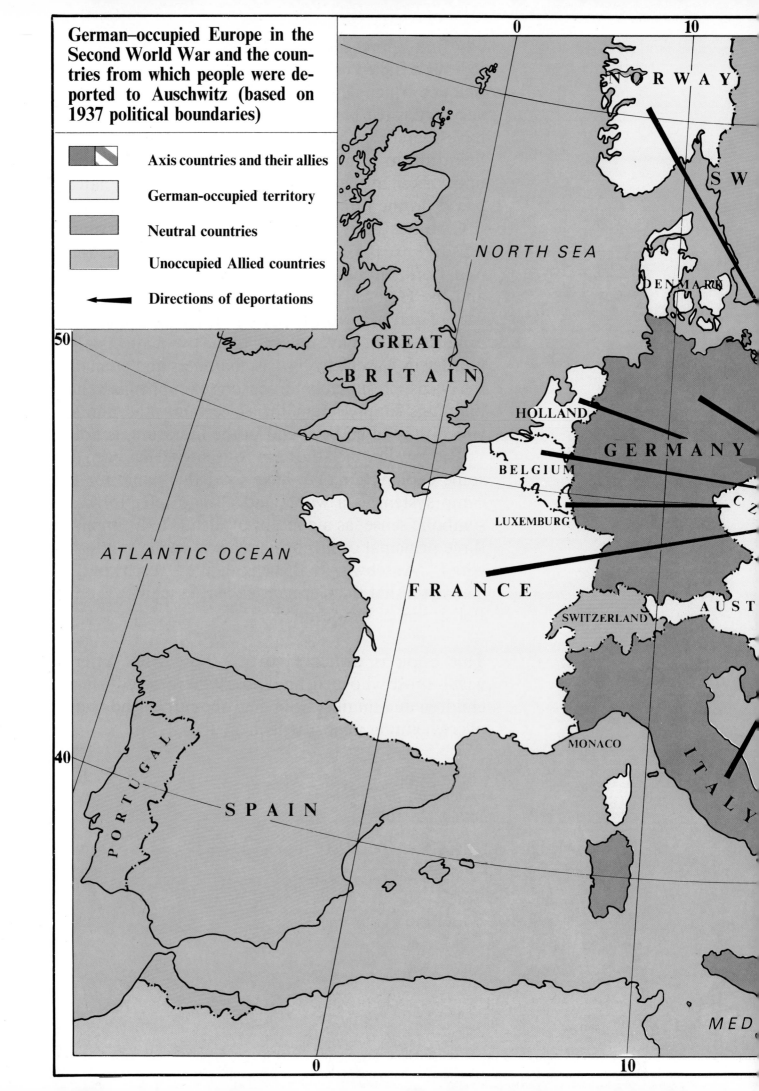

German–occupied Europe in the Second World War and the countries from which people were deported to Auschwitz (based on 1937 political boundaries)

Axis countries and their allies

German-occupied territory

Neutral countries

Unoccupied Allied countries

Directions of deportations

NORTH SEA

NORWAY

S W

DENMARK

GREAT BRITAIN

HOLLAND

BELGIUM

GERMANY

LUXEMBURG

C Z

ATLANTIC OCEAN

FRANCE

SWITZERLAND

AUST

50

MONACO

ITALY

40

PORTUGAL

SPAIN

MED

0

10

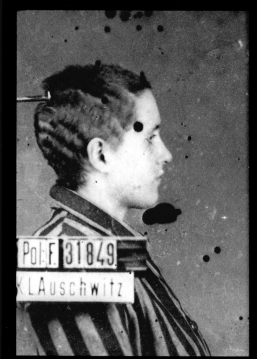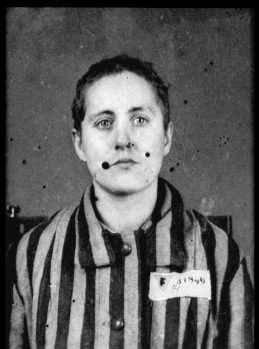

Above. Prisoner number 31849:
a French political prisoner who was
brought to Auschwitz on 27 January
1943. Name and fate unknown.

Opposite. Prisoner number 60460:
Edmund Fijałkowski, a Polish
political prisoner. He was brought to
Auschwitz on 21 August 1942 and
murdered on 1 March 1943 by means
of a phenol injection to the heart.

Auschwitz: The Nazi Murder Camp

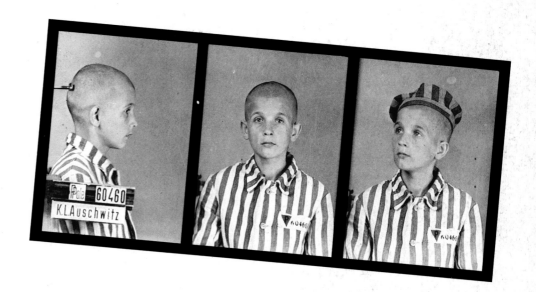

AUSCHWITZ was not the first Nazi concentration camp, but it was without doubt the most infamous. Although the concentration camp system had been in operation for seven years when Auschwitz opened on 14 June 1940, Auschwitz has come to symbolize the atrocities of the Nazi regime. There are several explanations for this, but one of the most valid is the enormous number of people who were murdered there—more than one million. Brought in trains (usually cattle cars and freight wagons) from all parts of occupied Europe, from as far away as Norway and Greece, the majority were murdered immediately on arrival. Most of the remainder died slowly, from starvation and the exhaustion of slave labour. The overwhelming majority of the victims—90 per cent—were Jewish, but others were murdered too: Poles, Gypsies, Soviet prisoners of war, Yugoslavs, homosexuals, and people of other ethnic and national groups and religions. Several hundred and sometimes more than a thousand people died every day. When the camp was liberated in 1945, only about 7,000 people were found alive. They were totally emaciated.

How had all this come about?

THE NAZI CONCENTRATION CAMP SYSTEM

Concentration camps were established in many places in the Third Reich almost as soon as the Nazis took power. Following an attempt to burn down the Reichstag, Paul von Hindenburg, the president of the Reich, issued an order at Hitler's insistence on 28 February 1933 which suspended civil liberties for an unspecified period and opened the way to the mass arrest of opponents of the Nazi party. Among the rights suspended were freedom of speech, freedom of the press, freedom of association and gathering, and the privacy of mail, telegrams, and telephones. Homes could be searched and property confiscated without recourse to the normal warrants. The Nazis also introduced 'protective imprisonment' (*Schutzhaft*), on the spurious grounds that the enemies of Nazism had to be isolated from the rest of German society in order to afford them 'protection' (*Schutz*) from public hostility. This was in effect imprisonment without trial. The first prisoners of the *Schutzhaftlager*—a term that was used interchangeably at the time with *Konzentrationslager*—were members of the Communist party, the Socialist party, and trade-unionists.

In 1933 alone, about fifty concentration camps were established in Germany. These included Berlin's 'Columbia Haus', Colditz,

Dachau, Hamburg-Fuhlsbüttel, Oranienburg, and Sonnenburg; throughout Germany, in fact, disused factory workshops and other sites were used for this purpose. These camps were originally staffed by police, SS, and Nazi storm troops (*Sturmabteilung*) but by July 1934, special units had been established; these were the SS-Totenkopfverbände. The authorities responsible for arresting prisoners and transporting them to the concentration camps were the Gestapo for political prisoners and the German criminal police for criminal offenders, but in 1939 these were merged to form the German national security office known as the Reichssicherheitshauptamt (RSHA).

Between 1936 and 1939, additional concentration camps were opened in Buchenwald, Flossenbürg, Ravensbrück (for women), and Sachsenhausen. All these camps were in Germany, and their prisoners, Jews and non-Jews, were all Germans. Following the annexation of Austria in 1938 a concentration camp was also opened in Mauthausen, for Austrians. With the invasion of Poland in 1939, Poles were also deported to these camps; citizens of other countries that came under Nazi rule were later sent to them too.

As the Nazis extended their grip on Europe, further concentration camps were established. Some of them were in Germany (Bergen-Belsen, Dora-Mittelbau, Gross-Rosen, Neuengamme, Niederhagen), and some in the newly occupied lands (Auschwitz, Natzweiler, Majdanek, Płaszów, Riga, Stutthof, Vaivara). Each camp had its own set of sub-camps, corresponding to the hundreds of factories, mines, foundries, and quarries where prisoners worked as slave labour. In addition to the concentration camps and their sub-camps, however, there were also camps that served exclusively for the mass murder of Jews: Bełżec, Kulmhof (Chełmno), Treblinka, and Sobibór, all in occupied Poland.

THE ESTABLISHMENT OF AUSCHWITZ

Auschwitz was the first Nazi concentration camp to be established in occupied Poland. The origins of the camp can be dated to early in 1940, when the SS sent a commission to Oświęcim to determine whether a set of barracks that had been constructed outside the town during the First World War and that between the wars had been used by the Polish military could be used as a concentration camp. Although the initial report was negative, a later inspection determined that the change of use would be possible after some construction work. Another commission, headed by SS-Hauptsturmführer Rudolf Höss, visited Oświęcim on 18–19 April 1940. Höss's report seems to have carried the most weight, for on 27 April 1940 SS-Reichsführer Heinrich Himmler ordered the establishment of a concentration camp in Oświęcim and on 4 May appointed Rudolf Höss its commandant.

THE NATIONAL ORIGINS OF AUSCHWITZ VICTIMS

Auschwitz was originally intended to serve as a concentration camp and a place of slow death for Polish political prisoners and other Poles. In later years, however, it gradually became the main centre for the systematic murder of those the Nazis considered human vermin, namely, Jews and Gypsies. The Nazis' pseudo-scientific theories on the superiority of the Aryan race condemned more than a million people to die in this one place alone.

The first prisoners to be sent to Auschwitz, a group of 728 Polish political prisoners (including a handful of Jews), arrived in Auschwitz from Tarnów on 14 June 1940. The first large group sent to Auschwitz from outside Poland was a transport of Czechs. This was in June 1941. Soviet prisoners of war started arriving a month later (immediately after the Nazi invasion of the Soviet Union), and groups from Yugoslavia in September 1941—initially men, but by July 1942 women as well. Among the latter were uniformed women partisans who demanded to be treated as prisoners of war and refused to have their heads shaved.

Within a few months of the Wannsee conference of January 1942, when the plan as to how to proceed with the murder of the Jews of Europe was presented—the 'Final Solution of the Jewish Question'—Auschwitz became the main camp to which Jews were sent to be murdered. The first known transport composed entirely of Jews arrived the very next month, and such transports continued to arrive from all over occupied Europe until November 1944.

In 1943 the Nazis started to murder Gypsies in Auschwitz. They brought them there for this purpose first from occupied Poland (from February 1943) and later from other countries, primarily from the Reich and from Bohemia and Moravia.

In this way, Auschwitz became the final destination for four main national and ethnic groups: Jews, who were by far the majority, Poles, Gypsies, and Soviet nationals. In addition, many Czechs, French nationals, Yugoslavs, Germans,

Austrians, and others were also imprisoned and murdered there.

The prisoner population of Auschwitz thus comprised many different kinds of people. Differences of national origin—and language—were compounded by a very wide range of social backgrounds, political commitments, and religious beliefs. For example, among the Jews were atheists and Communists as well as rabbis, and even Jews who had converted to Christianity.

ARRIVAL AT AUSCHWITZ

People were brought to Auschwitz from almost all over Europe. They were generally sent in overcrowded freight cars or cattle trucks, sometimes after having been tortured at Gestapo headquarters. Often they travelled for days without toilet facilities and with nothing to eat or drink.

Originally, the railway cars arrived at sidings near the camp; from May 1944 they continued into Auschwitz II-Birkenau itself, along a specially constructed spur. The majority of the people sent in these transports, especially the Jews, were murdered in gas chambers directly on arrival; their names never appeared in the camp records, so it is very difficult to determine precisely how many there were.

Those the SS deemed fit for work were not murdered immediately but were used as slave labour. They were given striped prison clothing and a prisoner number. Some groups of prisoners had their numbers tattooed on them; from 1943, most prisoners (though never Germans, unless they were Jewish) were tattooed with their numbers, generally on the left forearm. In all, more than 400,000 people, members of all the national and ethnic groups mentioned above, were allocated numbers, of whom about one-half died. Few lived longer than six months: they died from starvation, disease, the rigours of hard labour, beatings, torture, and summary execution—by shooting, hanging, or gassing.

CONDITIONS IN THE AUSCHWITZ
CONCENTRATION CAMP

Prisoners in Auschwitz I used for slave labour were housed in brick-built barracks. At first they slept on the floor but as the camp population grew, two- and three-tier bunk beds were installed. In Auschwitz II-Birkenau the prisoners were housed in brick or wooden huts. The wooden huts were constructed on the design for SS stables, and as many as 800 prisoners were sometimes crowded into a space designed for fifty-two horses. Lavatories were extremely primitive and few in number; prisoners had a very limited time to relieve themselves. Washing facilities were likewise grossly insufficient.

Changes of clothing and underwear were available only every few months; in the filthy conditions of the camp, clothes were always infested with lice. Periodic delousings not only gave no relief but were an additional torture: in summer the showers were scalding, in winter icy cold. Even in snow, prisoners had to run back to their blocks naked, only to find that the 'clean' clothes awaiting them there were also lice-infested. Such 'delousing' brought many dozens more patients to the overcrowded camp infirmary.

Virtually the only advantage of admission to the infirmary was that prisoners could in this way die in a bed; the only drugs available were aspirin and charcoal pills, making real medical treatment impossible. Prisoners called the infirmary the 'crematorium waiting-room': those whose recovery was too slow were murdered by a phenol injection administered to the heart or by being sent to the gas chamber.

The Daily Routine

At about 4.30 a.m., the morning gong sounded the start of an exceptionally long workday that was an unmitigated series of sufferings. At the sound of the gong, the prisoners in charge of each barrack—often prisoners who had been sent to Auschwitz for real crimes—ran among the plank beds, beating the prisoners with sticks to make them move faster. After a breakfast that consisted of half a litre of a lukewarm liquid that the SS called coffee, the prisoners were driven out to work.

'Work' meant slave labour in factories, mines, farming operations, and construction. Even the heaviest tasks, such as excavation and earth-moving, generally had to be done without equipment. Although prisoners were quite literally starving, they were often forced to carry bricks or push barrows at a run. Any attempt to rest was punished by transfer to special penal units where conditions were so very bad that few who experienced them survived.

The return from work was a terrible sight because the exhausted prisoners had to carry back to the camp the bodies of those who had died during work that day. Even dead bodies had to be present at the evening roll-call.[1]

The roll-call began immediately after the return from work. The number of prisoners could have been verified in little more than ten minutes, but the SS deliberately prolonged the roll-calls as an additional torment, particularly on days of heavy rain or sub-zero temperatures. Roll-calls generally lasted one hour, but sometimes they continued for many more. The roll-call on 6 July 1940 lasted nineteen hours, and that was not an isolated case. Such roll-calls naturally took their toll of prisoners' health, the more so because the prisoners often had to remain squatting throughout or else kneel on the ground with their arms raised. Those who fell over or let their hands drop would be shot or subjected to further sadistic treatment.

After the roll-call, prisoners got a meal which comprised a small piece of bread (300 grammes), some lard or margarine, and occasionally about 100 grammes of salted pork. Prisoners who had missed the noon meal because they had been been working outside the camp were given a soup as well, usually turnip or cabbage soup, but as it had been poured out at noon it was a cold and tasteless pulp by the evening.

Night brought little rest from the tortures of the day. The bunks were so overcrowded that prisoners were unable to move, and fleas and lice made rest impossible.

Punishments

Prisoners were totally at the mercy of the SS and could be sadistically punished at any time for infringement of camp rules that were completely arbitrary. For example, a starving prisoner who pulled out his gold teeth to exchange them for a piece of bread was punished, likewise a prisoner working in a garden who picked a few apples to satisfy his hunger. Prisoners could be punished if their beds were not made neatly, or even if they relieved themselves during working hours. The usual punishment for infringements of this kind was twenty-five or more lashes with a whip. An even more severe punishment was to twist prisoners' arms behind their backs, tie them with a rope, and suspend them for hours on end from a ceiling beam or post so that only the tips of their toes touched the floor.

Another frequent punishment was to confine prisoners in cells where conditions were particularly harsh. For example, prisoners

could be confined overnight four at a time in dark standing-ce[ll]
a metre square—a space so confined that it was impossible even [to]
sit down—which they had to enter on all fours, like a kennel. Th[e]
next morning, exhausted, they would be let out to work. Th[is]
could be repeated for nights on end.

Ventilation holes in all punishment cells were so small tha[t]
prisoners had trouble breathing; some were even asphyxiate[d].
There was one instance when 39 prisoners were crowded int[o]
a single cell: 20 died of suffocation, and 4 of the 19 survivors late[r]
died in the camp infirmary.

Executions

Prisoners working in the labour camp were always subject t[o]
summary execution. Some were shot, some were hanged, som[e]
were condemned to die of starvation; many were gassed.

The principal site in Auschwitz I where executions were carrie[d]
out was in the cells of Block 11 and its courtyard. This block[,]
known by prisoners as the 'block of death', contained punishmen[t]
cells in its cellars. The decision to shoot a prisoner could be mad[e]
by the Gestapo, by a visiting tribunal from Katowice, or by the S[S]
in the camp. Prisoners could even be shot arbitrarily during
'clear-outs' held when the cells of Block 11 were particularly
overcrowded. Shooting was also the rule for prisoners suspected of
involvement in resistance activities. Suspects would be held in
Block 11 while the camp Gestapo conducted 'investigations', which
always resulted in the prisoner being shot. The shootings took place
either in the yard of Block 11 or in ditches near the camp.

Prisoners were also executed at public hangings during the
evening roll-call. A portable gallows that generally stood in the
yard of Block 11 was carried out to the roll-call square for these
public executions. On 19 July 1943, twelve Polish prisoners were
hanged there on a specially made collective gallows. The last
public hangings took place in the men's camp on 30 December
1944, and in the women's camp on 6 January 1945.

From time to time, prisoners were also sentenced to die by
starvation, particularly when a collective punishment was meted
out as a 'reprisal' for another prisoner's escape. The *Lagerführer*
would arbitrarily select as many as ten or sometimes twenty
prisoners in such cases. They would be held in a single cell in Block
11 and given neither food nor drink. An SS man would check
through a peep-hole whether the prisoners were still alive, and

every few days the cell would be opened and the dead bodies removed. This punishment was also imposed on prisoners who had tried to escape.

THE EXPANSION OF THE CAMP

Increasing the capacity of Auschwitz to supply slave labour was of prime importance to the Nazis; from the moment the camp was established, prisoners were employed in expanding it. Whereas in 1940 Auschwitz had 20 buildings, of which 6 had only one storey, by 1942 there were 28 buildings of which all had more than one storey. The capacity of the barracks doubled in terms of cubic metres, but the number of prisoners quadrupled.

At this time it was realized that the capacity of Auschwitz could be expanded no further within the original site. Construction of twenty two-storey buildings was therefore initiated in an adjacent area, a development (the *Schutzhaftlagererweiterung*) that was to extend the camp as far as the main railway station in Oświęcim. Work also commenced on a programme of construction that envisaged a series of extensions designed to accommodate up to 200,000 people at a site two miles away in Brzezinka (Birkenau); this would become the Auschwitz II-Birkenau sub-camp. In 1941, Himmler ordered that no effort should be spared to make the SS the leading supplier of labour to the armament industry. In order to achieve this, an additional Auschwitz camp was established in 1942 in Monowice (Auschwitz III-Monowitz), a few miles east of Oświęcim, which sent prisoners, both men and women, to forty sub-camps established in factories and mines in Upper Silesia and even in the Sudetenland. The three main camps of Auschwitz— that is, Auschwitz I, Auschwitz II-Birkenau, and Auschwitz III-Monowitz—thus became one huge slave-labour complex. It brought the Third Reich high profits. For example, a payment of 12 million marks was made in 1943 in return for seven months' work by male prisoners and nine months' work by female prisoners in industrial plants.

THE MASS MURDER OF THE JEWS OF EUROPE

During its history Auschwitz served two functions: as a concentration camp for the slow death of different kinds of prisoners from hunger and slave labour, and as one of the principal centres for the mass murder of the Jews of Europe.

The first transport consisting entirely of Jews brought to be murdered in Auschwitz arrived in February 1942, only one month after the conference in Wannsee, from German Upper Silesia. It was followed by transports of Jews from Slovakia and France (starting March 1942); from Poland (starting May 1942); from Holland (starting July 1942); from Belgium and Yugoslavia (starting August 1942); from Bohemia and Moravia (starting October 1942); from Norway (starting December 1942); from Greece (starting March 1943); from Italy (starting October 1943); and from Hungary (starting April 1944). In total, more than a million Jews were brought to Auschwitz to be murdered.

The technique of industrialized mass murder had been planned methodically from the outset, even before the decision how to implement it had been formally adopted in January 1942. First, a method had to be chosen. Adolf Eichmann, the head of the department of the SS responsible for implementing the so-called 'Final Solution of the Jewish Question', discussed the matter with Rudolf Höss in the summer of 1941. Shooting, they felt, had to be ruled out because of the sheer numbers of people, and because of the emotional and psychological burden it would place on the SS who had to carry it out, notably in the context of the mass murder of women and children; on both counts, gassing was thought preferable. And so experiments were conducted: in September 1941, 600 Soviet prisoners of war and 250 Poles were taken from the camp infirmary and murdered with Zyklon B gas in the basement of Block 11.

Reflecting some years later on the experiments in the basement of Block 11 and later in Gas Chamber and Crematorium I, Höss said:

> At the time I did not think about the problem of killing Soviet prisoners of war. It was an order and I had to execute it. However, I will say frankly that killing that group of people by gas relieved my anxieties. It would soon be necessary to start the mass extermination of the Jews, and until that moment neither I nor Eichmann had known how to conduct a mass killing. A sort of gas was to be used, but it was not known what kind of gas was meant and how to use it. Now we had both the gas and the way of using it. I had always been concerned at the thought of mass shootings, particularly of women and children. I was already sick of executions. Now my mind was at ease.[2]

Thus Zyklon B came to be used as the instrument of murder. Höss reported that by introducing Zyklon B into the large

[2] Taken from testimony collected during Höss's investigation (Archives of the Auschwitz State Museum, *Proces Hössa* (The trial of Höss), xxi. 34).

Map of the Main Railways Used for Deporting Jews to Auschwitz

From Martin Gilbert, *Atlas of the Holocaust* (London: Dent, 1993).
Reproduced with the kind permission of the author.

underground chambers constructed for this purpose, about 1,500 people could be 'disposed of' at one time. This, he said, would require between 5 and 7 kilogrammes of Zyklon B. The whole operation was conceptualized as a sanitary procedure for exterminating human vermin. SS orderlies who had trained as 'fumigators' at Degesch (Deutsche Gesellschaft für Schädlingsbekämpfung)—the Hamburg pest control company that manufactured Zyklon B—poured the Zyklon B pellets into the gas chambers through special ducts. The records of Degesch show that about 20 tons of the material were delivered to Auschwitz in 1942 and 1943, for which payment was made by the SS.

The rather innocuous term 'gas chamber' thus in fact denotes a technological facility for mass murder. Auschwitz had gas chambers of different sizes, and in the largest of these as many as 2,000 people (even more than Höss had stated) could be murdered in 10 to 20 minutes. The first gas chamber, which was in Auschwitz I, was much smaller, having been improvised in the mortuary of the camp's crematorium. Additional improvised gas chambers were then operated in two small farmhouses in Auschwitz II-Birkenau, known as the 'white house' and the 'red house'. Then four custom-built gas chambers were constructed in Auschwitz II-Birkenau (Gas Chambers II, III, IV, and V), two beneath ground level and two above ground. Their main victims were Jews, transported to Auschwitz from all over Europe to be gassed. The pace of the murders reached a maximum in the summer of 1944, when more than 400,000 Jews were brought from Hungary over a period of two months and most of them were gassed immediately on arrival. In order to speed up the process, a spur of the railway line was extended right into Auschwitz II-Birkenau, directly adjacent to the gas chambers.

Murder of this magnitude presented the SS with the murderer's classic problem on an unprecedented scale: the disposal of the bodies. Each of the four custom-built gas chambers in Auschwitz II-Birkenau had its own crematorium, giving a combined theoretical capacity (following the manufacturers' specifications) of reducing 4,416 bodies to ashes every twenty-four hours. In practice, however, 8,000 bodies could be disposed of if the incinerators were emptied before the corpses were fully reduced to ashes and any remaining bones pulverized separately. But even this was far fewer than the number of people that could be murdered in a day. The solution adopted was to pile up the surplus bodies and burn them in the open air. Up to 2,000 bodies would be piled up, doused with methanol wastes, and set fire to: in twenty-four hours nothing remained but ashes, which were then scattered on fields or dumped into nearby ponds or the Soła and Vistula rivers.

German war interests required the maximization of economic benefits from this cold-blooded murder. Accordingly, before the bodies were burned the victims' hair was cut off and fillings and false teeth made of precious metals were removed. The hair was used to manufacture haircloth, and the metals were melted into bars and sent to Berlin. After the liberation, seven tons of hair were found in the camp's warehouses; the Nazis had not had time to process it all. Proof that this hair came from victims of gassing was subsequently provided by the Cracow Institute of Judicial Expertise, whose analyses showed that traces of prussic acid, a poisonous component typical of Zyklon compounds, were present in the hair. But even without such analyses, the presence of hair-grips in the hair was indication enough that the hair had been cut from corpses. Similar tests on bales of haircloth taken from Auschwitz showed that human hair, probably female hair, had been used in its manufacture.

Property brought to the camp by the prisoners was systematically looted, an operation for which more than thirty warehouses were set aside in a special compound within the camp, known by the prisoners as 'Canada'. Höss's memoirs record that prisoners worked day and night to sort the booty. Freight cars were loaded every day for shipment back into the Reich—generally between five and ten, and sometimes as many as twenty—but heaps of baggage still remained to be sorted.

RESISTANCE IN AUSCHWITZ

The moment the camp gate closed behind the prisoners in the labour camp they became involved in a continuous struggle for life and human dignity. In some prisoners, this forged a determination to tell the world the truth about SS crimes, and to fight the Nazi regime in any way possible. Since nothing could be done openly, all kinds of ingenious clandestine tactics were devised.

Resistance in the camp was largely disorganized and spontaneous, and involved many different kinds of prisoners, but over the course of time various organized resistance groups emerged also, including those led by Polish nationalists associated with the Polish Home Army and those led by prisoners of Polish and other nationalities, consisting mainly of socialists and Communists. Resistance activities were many and varied. Ways were developed to save prisoners in danger, get drugs and give medical assistance, and keep up prisoners' spirits. Escapes had to be organized in such a way that other prisoners would not be punished. Evidence of Nazi crimes had to be collected and smuggled out in coded notes hidden in clothes or other objects specially prepared for this purpose, or buried in the ground in the hope that they could be recovered when circumstances permitted. One was found as recently as 1980, written by a Greek Jew who had been a member of the Sonderkommando—the detachments of Jewish prisoners who were forced to empty the gas chambers and burn the corpses. Groups of the Sonderkommando were themselves murdered at regular intervals because of their intimate knowledge of Nazi atrocities.

The Sonderkommando have a special place in the history of resistance in Auschwitz because they organized the only significant revolt to take place in Auschwitz. In October 1944, one of the last of these groups, knowing what their fate would be, decided to organize a revolt. Four Jewish women smuggled explosives to them, and they succeeded in destroying Gas Chamber and Crematorium IV and killing some SS guards. The women were caught and hanged, but in consequence of their action one of the four murder installations functioning in Auschwitz at that time was rendered inoperative.

THE EVACUATION AND LIBERATION OF AUSCHWITZ

In January 1945 it became clear that Soviet troops were approaching, and the Nazis hastily tried to evacuate the camp. By the time of the last roll-call, on 18 January, they had moved some 60,000 prisoners out of Auschwitz and its sub-camps, mainly on foot, with the intention of transferring them to concentration camps deeper in the Reich. Only those who were too sick to march were left behind. The prisoners were escorted by armed SS and very often had to carry SS baggage; those unable to continue were shot. The SS had planned to shoot all the prisoners who had been left behind too, but the Soviet advance was so rapid that they were unable to do so.

The day after the liberation of Auschwitz, a special Soviet commission began to investigate the crimes committed there and to gather documentary evidence. It was on the basis of this material that the International Military Tribunal in Nuremberg branded the activities of the Nazi concentration camps, and chief among them those perpetrated at Auschwitz, as crimes against humanity.

AFTERWORD

It is almost impossible to present what happened in Auschwitz using ordinary, everyday language. It was not an everyday place. The events and the sheer quantity defy the imagination. Can the pain caused by the death of hundreds of thousands of people be measured? Can the human mind visualize murder on a mass scale, conceived and implemented as a technological process and measured by the productivity of gas chambers and crematorium incinerators? If we who witnessed the atrocities of the Second World War are unable today to convey our memories of the past in an adequate manner, how much more difficult it will be for future generations to comprehend the full horror of the term born of that war: genocide.

Even though more than forty-five years have elapsed since the defeat of Nazism, our duty remains to reveal the atrocities perpetrated in its name. Millions of people—Jews, Poles, Gypsies, Soviet citizens, and others—lost their lives, and millions more suffered—their children and grandchildren continue to bear the scars to this day.

In ten or twenty years from now, virtually all the eye-witnesses of the atrocities of Nazism will be dead. The world will be populated by generations who were not alive during the Second World War and did not experience it personally. They might be tempted to say, 'Such are the laws of nature. Is it not better to forget? Is it not better to wipe that period from our memory? Is it not better simply to be silent about things we have not experienced?' The answer to such questions is an emphatic 'No!'

We remember not in order to open old wounds, not to fill the imagination of the young with images of horror: we remember as part of our homage to the victims. If we fail to remember, then their suffering and death will have no meaning: history will be incomplete.

Kazimierz Smoleń

[27]

Opposite. Prisoner number 26947:
Katarzyna Kwoka, a Polish political
prisoner who was brought to
Auschwitz on 13 December 1942
from Zamość and died there on
6 February 1943, probably from
typhus.

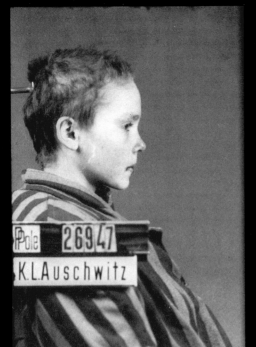
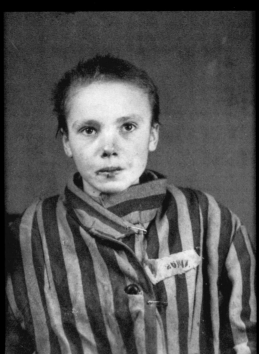

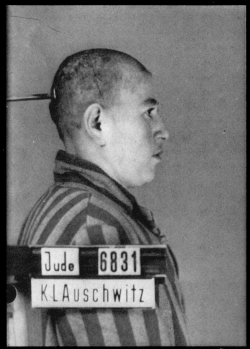

Above. Prisoner number 6831:
a Jewish woman who was brought to
Auschwitz on 27 April 1942 from
Cracow. Name and fate unknown.

Opposite. Prisoner number 63040:
Szija (Shaya) Kleinmann, a Jew
brought to Auschwitz on
4 September 1942. Fate unknown.

Previous page. Photograph taken
after the liberation of the camp.
(Photo taken from the Soviet film
*Chronicle of the Liberation of
Auschwitz, 1945*)

Auschwitz
in Documentary
Photographs

DOCUMENTARY photographs of Auschwitz, the largest of the Nazi mass-murder complexes, are an important source of evidence of Nazi war crimes and of the fate of the vast numbers of people who died there.

A small selection of such photographs was published by the Museum in 1980 but the scope of the present selection is far wider, principally because two major new collections have been acquired since then. One of these comprises aerial photographs taken by the Allies in 1944 and January 1945, while the other comprises about 500 photographs taken by the Zentralbauleitung (the Central Construction Office of the SS) to record the process of the camp's development. These two collections therefore added a new dimension to the Museum's photographic archives.

The photographs reproduced here include material from these new collections as well as from the archives of the camp Gestapo. In addition, there are clandestine photographs taken by members of resistance organizations, some of which survived and found their way to the Museum archives, and photographs taken when the camp was liberated and in the months that followed. Finally, there are photographs of Auschwitz as it is today.

To comprehend fully the photographs that are included in this album, it is useful to know more about how, why, and by whom they were taken, and how they survived and made their way to the Museum archives. Each of the various sources is therefore considered in more detail below.

NAZI PHOTOGRAPHS

The Nazis wanted to record what they were doing, but on the other hand they were aware that photographs of concentration camps would be damning evidence of their crimes. Accordingly, and in compliance with the general directives of SS-Reichsführer Heinrich Himmler and the Inspectorate of Concentration Camps, the Auschwitz authorities sought to forbid unauthorized photography of anything connected with the camp, directly or indirectly. Order No. 4/43, dated 2 February 1943 and signed by the camp's commandant, SS-Obersturmbannführer Rudolf Höss, was explicit on this. Item 3 reads: 'I want to point out once more that taking pictures in the camp is forbidden. I shall punish with the utmost severity those who do not observe this order.'[1] The only exception was for official photographs specifically authorized.

[1] Archives of the Auschwitz State Museum (APMO), Orders issued by Auschwitz Headquarters.

[34]

At first, all photographs were made in a single laboratory known as the Erkennungsdienst (Reconnaissance Service) which was supervised by the Political Section—that is, the camp Gestapo. The head of the laboratory was SS-Hauptscharführer Bernhardt Walter and his assistant was SS-Unterscharführer Ernst Hofmann. The whole operation of developing the film, fixing the negatives, and printing photographs and enlargements was generally done by a team of ten to twelve prisoners. This process was supervised by SS men to ensure that the negatives and prints did not fall into the wrong hands. The finished photographs were handed over to the authorized recipients and their delivery was recorded; duplicate and defective prints were scrupulously destroyed. Highly sensitive pictures—for example, those of executions or of the burning of bodies—were developed by the SS men themselves; the most incriminating were printed only in a single copy, and the negatives would be destroyed when they had been handed over to the commandant.

A major part of the photographs in the Museum are contact prints of headshots of prisoners: about 38,000, or just under 10 per cent of the people who were registered in the concentration camp for forced labour. In this context, perhaps it needs to be restated that Auschwitz had two functions: it was the largest of the Nazi concentration camps used as an instrument of terror and for forced labour, and later in the war it became the main centre to which Jews were deported to be murdered. Prisoners sent to Auschwitz in order to be interned there were registered and received prisoner numbers; until 1943, most were also photographed. These photographs comprised part of the camp records and were numbered consecutively. The majority are of Polish prisoners, since prisoners were photographed systematically only during the first years of the camp's existence, when it was used mainly for Poles. Jews sent straight to the gas chambers on arrival were not registered, had no prisoner numbers, and were not photographed. Of the relatively few Jews who were selected on arrival as being fit for forced labour, only a very small proportion were photographed. The consequence is that there are therefore very few headshots of Jewish prisoners in Auschwitz; many of those which do exist are of Jews who happened to have been among groups of political prisoners sent to Auschwitz before 1942.

The practice of photographing prisoners was largely discontinued in 1943, except for particular groups of newcomers: Germans, for example, were photographed until the very end. The Erkennungsdienst also took photographs of captured partisans; of prisoners shot while trying to escape; of prisoners who committed suicide rather than face torture; and of the effects of medical experiments conducted on prisoners by SS doctors. However, except for the latter category, virtually none of these photographs have survived. Jews considered particularly 'interesting' because of their physical features or dress were also brought to the Erkennungsdienst to be photographed from time to time.

When the Nazis evacuated Auschwitz, they tried to destroy the photographs. Bronisław Jureczek, a former Polish political prisoner, described how the photographs survived:

At almost the last moment we were ordered to burn all the negatives and photographs which were in the Erkennungsdienst. First, we put wet photographic paper and also photographs and then a large number of photographs and negatives into a tile stove in such large numbers as to block the exhaust outlet. This ensured that when we set fire to the materials in the stove only the photographs and negatives near the stove door would be consumed, and that the fire would later die out due to the lack of air. After the war I learned that our assumption had been right, and that a high percentage of the photographs and negatives had survived and found their way into the right hands . . . Moreover, under the pretext of haste, I had deliberately scattered a number of photographs and negatives in the rooms of the lab. I knew that with the hurried evacuation of the camp, no one would have time to gather them all and that something would survive.[2]

Supervision of the laboratory by the camp Gestapo was very strict because the photographs were considered top secret; even the slightest suspicion of a prisoner could result in a death sentence. Even so, prisoners working in the Gestapo photographic laboratory risked their lives many times to smuggle material out of the camp. According to Alfred Woycicki, another Pole who had worked in the laboratory:

Original photographs showing equipment and various scenes in the camp were sent out several times. In one case, they were pictures taken by someone in the women's section in Birkenau. I do not know the photographer's name. He was a Hauptscharführer who had been especially sent [to Auschwitz II-Birkenau] for this purpose by order of the RSHA. That was late in 1943 or early in 1944. The camp was informed about his arrival . . . He took

[2] Ibid., Testimonies of Former Prisoners, xix. 31.

[36]

a number of pictures in the women's camp and then brought them to the Erkennungsdienst on the same day to have them developed so he could decide if the pictures were good. Because of that, I saw all the pictures. Their contents so incriminated the camp authorities that I could not understand why they had been taken. One of the photographs showed a pile of female bodies . . . Another showed the infirmary for women. Patients lay in total disorder; several were naked and clearly exhausted.[3]

[3] Ibid., The Trial of Höss, vii. 4.

Woycicki later testified that in spite of the exceptional vigilance of the SS he had managed to make one print of each photograph, and that these were then smuggled out of the camp. Unfortunately, like many other photographs smuggled out of the camp, they have disappeared.

The Murder of the Jews of Hungary: How the Evidence Survived

The best known of the SS photographs are those taken to record the arrival of Jews from Hungary at Auschwitz II-Birkenau in 1944, the SS doctors' selection of those to be murdered immediately by gassing, and how the victims actually went to their deaths in the gas chambers. What is less well known is how these photographs survived.

The photographs come from an album found after the war by a Jewish survivor of Auschwitz named Lili Jacob (later Zelmanovic, now Meier).[4] She came originally from Bilke, a small Slovak town annexed by Hungary in 1939. The Jews of Bilke were forcibly relocated to the ghetto in Berehovo, and on 24 May 1944 they were deported from Berehovo to Auschwitz II-Birkenau. When their train arrived there after an exhausting two-day journey, they had to undergo the life-or-death selection conducted on the railway ramp by the SS doctors. Lili, then 18 years old, her three elder brothers, and her father survived the selection. They were designated by the SS doctors as fit for work and were sent off for forced labour rather than to their deaths in the gas chambers of Auschwitz II-Birkenau. Other family members, including her mother, two younger brothers, and more distant relatives, were not so lucky.[5] In fact, Lili Jacob was the only one of that group to survive.

[4] Correspondence between the Museum and Lili Zelmanovic (1961), ibid., Photographs, ia. 85.

At the end of the war, Lili Jacob was in the Nordhausen-Dora camp, sick with typhus and in the camp hospital. Along with other sick prisoners she was rehoused by the liberating army in barracks that had formerly housed the SS. In searching the barracks for

[5] Serge Klarsfeld, 'Introduction', *The Auschwitz Album: Lili Jacob's Album* (New York, 1980).

winter clothing, Lili came across a photograph album. In the album she found photographs of concentration camp prisoners, including—by a remarkable coincidence—photographs not only of members of her family who had been murdered in Auschwitz II-Birkenau, but also of herself in a roll-call of new women prisoners. Not surprisingly, she decided to keep the album.

After the war, Lili Jacob lived for a time in Czechoslovakia. In 1946, in desperate need of money, she attempted to sell the album to representatives of the Jewish community in Prague. They could not afford her price, but eventually she agreed to let them make negatives from the photographs in return for a smaller payment. Thirty were subsequently reproduced in a book entitled *The Tragedy of Slovak Jews* which was published in Bratislava in 1949.

For several years thereafter, the negatives remained unused. In 1955, two Czech researchers who had themselves been in Auschwitz, Ota Kraus and Erich Kulka, were going through the archives of a Prague museum looking for material for a book when they came across two packets labelled 'Photographs from Auschwitz'. The packets contained 203 glass negatives in a 5 x 7-in. format, and they recognized them as being photographs of Auschwitz II-Birkenau.[6] Knowing that in order to identify them properly they would have to go to Poland, they contacted a former Auschwitz prisoner in Poland for assistance. The person they contacted was Józef Cyrankiewicz, the Polish premier; and at his invitation they went to the Auschwitz Museum taking sixty-four of the negatives with them.

Careful examination of the photographs in the Museum by Professor Jan Sehn and two former Auschwitz prisoners, Kazimierz Smoleń and Dawid Szmulewski, confirmed their opinion. In an official note written on 22 November 1956 they stated: 'Having analysed carefully the contents of the reproductions, we have come to the conclusion that, with the exception of two photographs, all the others are prints of photographs made when great numbers of Jewish people were getting off at the railroad siding in Brzezinka [Auschwitz II-Birkenau].'[7] One set of these photographs was given to the Auschwitz Museum and another to Yad Vashem in Israel. However, the origin of the photographs was unknown, beyond the fact that a woman in Prague had permitted negatives to be made in 1946.

Lili Jacob had meanwhile emigrated to the United States, taking the album with her. In 1961, in connection with the trial of Adolf Eichmann, an interview with her (now Lili Zelmanovic) was

[6] Erich Kulka correspondence, APMO, Photographs, *ia.* 54.

[7] A formal note dated 22 Nov. 1956; ibid. 1.

published in the United States in *Parade* magazine in which she described how she had found the album and explained that she still had it in her possession. When the Auschwitz Museum learned of the interview, they wrote to her and asked for more details. Her reply provided the information that has been given here.

The negatives found by Kraus and Kulka played an important role in the pre-trial investigations in connection with the trial in Frankfurt in 1963–5 of twenty-two former SS men from Auschwitz. When the existence of the original album was made known, Lili Jacob was herself invited to testify in Frankfurt, bringing the album with her.

The photos served to identify a former Blockführer, Baretzky, as one of the SS men present at the selection of Jews at the railway ramp. During this trial, Bernhardt Walter, former head of the Gestapo photographic laboratory, was questioned as to who had taken the photographs. During pre-trial investigations by the German prosecutor's office, he had admitted that he had run a photographic laboratory in Auschwitz, but said that his only task had been to photograph the newly arrived prisoners sent to him in Auschwitz I. When he was shown photographs taken on the ramp in Auschwitz II-Birkenau he denied having taken them. He claimed that he had visited Auschwitz II-Birkenau only once, to take a panoramic view of the camp from the main guardhouse watch-tower, and that he had received the order to do so from Berlin. Questioned again, he admitted that he had heard talk of a 'ramp', but denied that he had ever heard the term 'selection'. Asked who might have taken the pictures, he was unable to give a definite answer but said that it could have been Ernst Hofmann, his assistant. Later he admitted having seen in the drying room of the laboratory photographs of groups of Jews that could perhaps have come from a set of pictures taken at the ramp. While he admitted that he had taken photographs of Jews brought to the Erkennungsdienst because their physical features or dress were considered particularly interesting, he again stressed that he had never taken pictures outside Auschwitz I, and repeated that Hofmann had been one of the 'outside' photographers. He did not question the authenticity of the photographs. He even admitted that they were official photographs, and that they could not have been taken from a hiding place.[8]

During the trial, Walter continued to deny that he had ever been at the ramp. Baretzky accused him of lying and said that he had often seen him at the ramp riding a BMW motor cycle. Walter

[8] Klarsfeld, 'Introduction', 34.

initially denied the accusation, claiming that he had had a smaller motor cycle; later he confessed that he had been at the ramp but had not said so earlier because he had not understood the questions of the court.[9]

According to Hermann Langbein's account of the trial, Walter eventually admitted he had taken photographs at the ramp;[10] however, in introductions to two books published almost simultaneously, Serge Klarsfeld and Peter Hellman both said that Walter was adamant to the very end that he had not taken the pictures.[11] It is quite obvious that the photographs could have been taken only by an SS man authorized to do so: it could have been Walter, Hofmann acting with Walter's knowledge, or both of them. The latter seems the most probable. Bronisław Jureczek, the former Polish prisoner mentioned earlier as having worked in the laboratory, said in his testimony, 'Boss Walter also took pictures of prisoners coming to Auschwitz by train.'[12] Wilhelm Brasse, another former prisoner who had worked in the laboratory, said that 'Hofmann used to replace Walter in supervising prisoners at work, and like Walter, used to leave that place in order to take pictures outside.'[13] When Brasse saw the photographs from the album he asserted: 'Some [photographs] were taken by Walter, some by Hofmann, and some were reproduced from a film delivered personally by the camp commandant, Rudolf Höss. The photographs were placed in the album by Myszkowski, a prisoner working in the Erkennungsdienst; he decorated the album and wrote captions for the photographs. The album was made for the camp commandant.'[14]

Bauleitung Photographs

At the end of 1941 or the beginning of 1942, a second photographic laboratory was established in Auschwitz. This was operated by the Central Construction Office of the SS (Zentralbauleitung der Waffen SS) and was known as the Bauleitung laboratory.

The Bauleitung laboratory was under the direction of Dietrich Kamann, an SS man responsible for photographic documentation of the construction work in Auschwitz and its surroundings to supplement the Construction Office's written reports. Originally the Erkennungsdienst laboratory had been responsible for this, but because the staff there objected to doing location work in all weathers it was hard for Kamann to maintain the necessary

[9] Hermann Langbein, *Der Auschwitz Prozess: Eine Dokumentation* (Vienna, 1965), 314.

[10] Ibid.

[11] Klarsfeld, 'Introduction'; Peter Hellman, 'Introduction', *The Auschwitz Album: A Book Based upon an Album Discovered by a Concentration Camp Survivor, Lili Meier* (New York, 1981).

[12] APMO, Testimonies of Former Prisoners, iii. 405.

[13] Ibid. 378.

[14] Ibid. 382.

records. Ludwik Lawin, a Polish prisoner employed in arranging the photographs in albums to record the progress of construction, suggested to Kamann that he set up a separate photographic unit in the camp's construction office.[15] The idea appealed to Kamann: having his own photographic unit would make him indispensable and help prevent him being sent to the front. He set about obtaining the necessary authorization and rapidly succeeded.

[15] Ibid. cxiv. 139.

The majority of the Bauleitung photographs were taken in 1943, the year when building activity in Auschwitz II-Birkenau was at its peak. They provide a solid record of the very many types of construction undertaken: barracks for prisoners, drainage ditches, workshops and storage facilities, gas chambers and crematoria, and other buildings.

Lawin decided to keep some of the photographs he was supposed to be pasting into albums for Kamann—many of which had figured in Bauleitung progress reports, had been enlarged for display on the Bauleitung bulletin boards, or used in albums presented to SS dignitaries—so that he would have documentary evidence of Nazi atrocities. He later wrote:

> I found it relatively easy to persuade Kubiak, a prisoner working as an assistant in the laboratory, to make contact prints from many negatives . . . I mean photographs which in my opinion had a higher value than those connected with construction. I gave one set of prints to Dubiel [a prisoner assigned to work as a gardener]; I wanted him to have them in case I didn't survive.[16]

[16] Ibid. xxxi. 74.

Unfortunately those photographs have disappeared. However, Lawin buried another set of photographs beneath a waste dump near the Construction Office and took care to remember the place he had chosen. On 25 September 1946, a flask containing negatives of fifty-two photographs taken at Auschwitz was found buried in the exact spot Lawin had specified, fourteen paces from the third barrack used by the Construction Office.

In 1981, the Auschwitz Museum received from Yad Vashem in Jerusalem about 500 negatives of photographs from an album called *Bauleitung*. The majority showed the construction and expansion of the camp and buildings in the vicinity of Auschwitz; some were identical to the photographs hidden by Lawin. The album had reached Yad Vashem via the Jewish community of Berlin, having probably been turned over to them by a Soviet general in October 1945. It had been carefully looked after by a member of the community, Heinz Cols, but in 1975 he had suggested giving it to a museum in Jerusalem. It was ultimately acquired by Yad Vashem, which later gave a set of the photographs to the Auschwitz Museum.

CLANDESTINE PHOTOGRAPHS

Another documentary source of evidence on Auschwitz is photographs taken illegally by members of underground organizations. The Museum's collection includes clandestine photographs of the first transport of prisoners, photographs of prisoners who had escaped, and photographs taken when the camp was evacuated.

Of particular significance are three pictures taken by prisoners from the Sonderkommando, the special unit made up of Jewish prisoners that was responsible for burning the bodies of people who had been gassed. They were smuggled out to Cracow via the Polish Socialist Party in Brzeszcze, a small town near Auschwitz, with the purpose of documenting SS atrocities and identifying their perpetrators. The accompanying note, dated 4 September 1944, was written by Józef Cyrankiewicz and Stanisław Kłodziński, Polish political prisoners who belonged to the camp resistance movement. They explained that these were photographs from Auschwitz II-Birkenau of people going to be gassed and of the burning of bodies. One photograph showed women running naked in the open air after having been told to undress, allegedly for a bath, but in fact before being driven to the gas chamber. Another showed a heap of bodies piled outdoors; they explained that bodies were burned outdoors when the crematorium could not keep pace with the numbers to be burned.[17] Alter Fajnzylberg, a Jew from France who had worked in the Sonderkommando, later described how the pictures were taken:

> Also in that period, namely somewhere about midway through 1944, we decided to take pictures secretly to record our work: that is, [to record the] crimes committed by the Germans in the Auschwitz gas chambers. In order to do that, it was necessary to get a good camera and film. I do not remember precisely all the details, but we actually managed to get such a camera . . . Having decided to take such pictures, I was unable to operate entirely alone. From the very beginning, several prisoners from our Sonderkommando were in on my secret: Szlomo Dragon, his brother Josek Dragon, and Alex, a Greek Jew whose surname I do not remember.
>
> On the day on which the pictures were taken—I do not

[17] Ibid., Materials of the Camp's Resistance Movement, ii. 136.

remember the day or the month exactly—we allocated tasks. Some of us were to guard the person taking the pictures. In other words, we were to keep a careful watch for the approach of anyone who did not know the secret, and above all for any SS men moving about in the area. At last the moment came. We all gathered at the western entrance leading from the outside to the gas chamber of Crematorium V: we could not see any SS men in the watch-tower overlooking the door from above the barbed wire, nor near the place where the pictures were to be taken. Alex, the Greek Jew, quickly took out his camera, pointed it toward a heap of burning bodies, and pressed the shutter. This is why the photograph shows prisoners from the Sonderkommando working at the heap. One of the SS was standing beside them, but his back was turned towards the crematorium building. Another picture was taken from the other side of the building, where women and men were undressing among the trees. They were from a transport that was to be murdered in the gas chamber of Crematorium V.

Describing this event, I want to emphasize once again that when these pictures were taken, all the prisoners I mentioned were present. In other words, even though the Greek Jew, Alex, was the person who actually pressed the shutter, one can say that the pictures were taken by all of us. Today, I cannot remember what the camera looked like, because I had never taken pictures before and I did not hold the camera, but I think it looked like a German Leica.[18]

[18] Ibid., Declaration, cxiv. 57–8.

AERIAL PHOTOGRAPHS

Analysis of the aerial photographs of Auschwitz taken by the Allies in 1944 and January 1945 and their interpretation in the interest of historical research was pioneered by two American researchers, Dino A. Brugioni and Robert G. Poirier. Working in the late 1970s, their assumption was that the many advances in equipment and techniques that had been developed at the National Photographic Interpretation Center in the United States since the Second World War would enable more information to be extracted from such pictures than had been possible at the time they were taken.

The researchers faced a problem in that because of the technical capacity of the cameras carried by Second World War aircraft, the coverage of aerial photography was limited to strategic or tactical targets rather than the wide-area coverage of modern photo-reconnaissance. Since the cameras would be switched on shortly before reaching the target and turned off as soon as the target was imaged, aerial photographs would have been taken only of concentration camps close to targets of military interest.

Fortunately for their research, Auschwitz was only a few kilometres from the large I. G. Farben factory set up in Monowitz for the manufacture of synthetic oil and rubber. It had been subjected to Allied air raids from 4 April 1944 to 21 January 1945, and during that period the Allies had taken pictures of the whole area.[19] Brugioni and Poirier's enlargement and subsequent analysis of these photographs provides evidence of camp buildings that no longer exist, having been partially or completely destroyed by the SS as they abandoned the camp: installations for mass murder—gas chambers with crematoria—as well as barracks for prisoners. A train, the railway ramp, and people being driven toward the gas chambers can also be seen.

The aerial photographs included in this volume come from a collection of photographs taken by the Allies that was recently presented to the Auschwitz–Birkenau State Museum by the United States Holocaust Memorial Museum.

LIBERATION AND POST-LIBERATION PHOTOGRAPHS

In considering the photographic history of Auschwitz, attention should also be given to photographs of the prisoners and camp buildings as they looked at the time of the liberation in 1945. Such photographs come from a variety of sources.

Some of the photographs reproduced in this book derive from a film entitled *Chronicle of the Liberation of Auschwitz*. They were taken by four film cameramen of the liberating Soviet army: N. Bykow, K. Kutub-Zade, A. Pawłow, and A. Woroncow. Filming took place over a period of several weeks and included many aspects of the process of liberation—for example, scenes of a mass funeral that was held late in February 1945. But it was a strange world that was being filmed at that moment, in the transition from the wartime reality of the concentration camp. The former prisoners were now free to roam where they wished within Auschwitz, and so they sometimes posed for the photographers in settings that would have been quite impossible during the existence of the camp. A famous example is the scene of a column of children walking between the once-electrified barbed-wire perimeter fences—a potent cinematographic image, but one that is to some extent surreal.

Some photographs come from a special commission of inves-

[19] Dino A. Brugioni and Robert C. Poirier, *The Holocaust Revisited: A Retrospective Analysis of the Auschwitz-Birkenau Extermination Complex* (Washington D.C., 1979).

tigation gathering evidence for the trials of Nazi war criminals and were taken by Henryk Makarewicz, a Polish soldier who came to Auschwitz in January 1945, immediately after the camp was liberated. Others were taken by Stanisław Mucha, a photographer with a Polish Red Cross team who visited Auschwitz from mid-February to mid-March 1945 and also took pictures for a Soviet commission investigating Nazi crimes in Auschwitz. Another set of photographs was made by Stanisław Łuczko, of the Cracow Institute of Judicial Expertise, who accompanied the inspection of Auschwitz by Professor Jan Sehn, as examining magistrate, from 11 to 25 May 1945. Finally there are pictures taken by Stanisław Kolowca, who accompanied a British delegation headed by the Dean of Canterbury Cathedral, Dr Hewlett Johnson, which inspected the camp on 29 May 1945.

In selecting photographs for publication in this volume, the aim has been to present all facets of the camp's history. Photographs have therefore been selected for their documentary significance, in some cases despite technical shortcomings: the photographers were not professionals, their equipment was frequently poor, and the weather conditions were often unsuitable. Where contemporary photographs were not available it has sometimes been necessary to use recent pictures, either of the original buildings or of installations reconstructed in accordance with the historical evidence.

Teresa Świebocka
and
Renata Bogusławska-Świebocka

1

View of the centre of Oświęcim. Under its German name of Auschwitz, the town became infamous as the location of the Nazi murder camp that operated from 1940 to 1945 and has entered history as the symbol of Nazi genocide. Auschwitz was a concentration camp for prisoners of various nationalities; from 1942 it gradually became the main centre for the Nazis' systematic murder of the Jews of Europe. The overwhelming majority of the people murdered in Auschwitz—90 per cent—were Jews. (Photographer unknown, 1939)

2

View of the barracks of Auschwitz when it was a Polish army camp, before the Second World War. In 1940 it was taken over by the SS and used as a concentration camp. This site, which now comprises part of the Auschwitz Museum, was later known variously as the *Stammlager* (base camp) and Auschwitz I. The three-storey building seen in the photograph housed the offices of the camp headquarters. The single-storey buildings where prisoners were held were surrounded by barbed-wire fences. (Photographer unknown, prior to 1 Sept. 1939)

1

2

3

4

[48]

3

Most of the Poles living near Auschwitz and in the neighbouring villages within an area of some 40 square kilometres were deported to allow for the establishment of a zone under the camp's authority (*Interessengebiet des Lagers*). (Photographer unknown, 1941)

4

Deportation of Polish farmers from the area of Brzezinka to permit construction of the second and largest section of the camp, Auschwitz II-Birkenau. (A. Gładyszek, 1941)

5

Auschwitz I and Auschwitz II-Birkenau. (Aerial photo taken by the Allies, 26 June 1944)

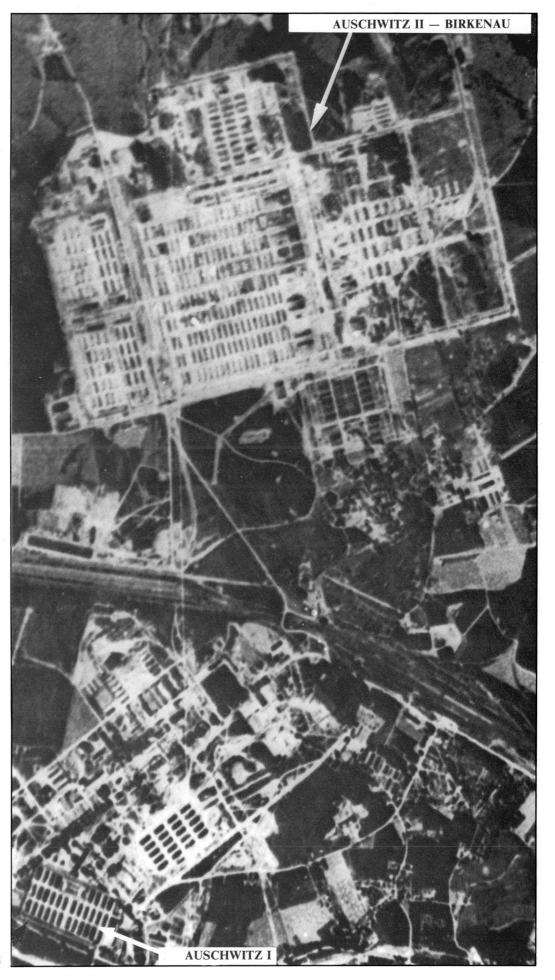

AUSCHWITZ II — BIRKENAU

AUSCHWITZ I

5

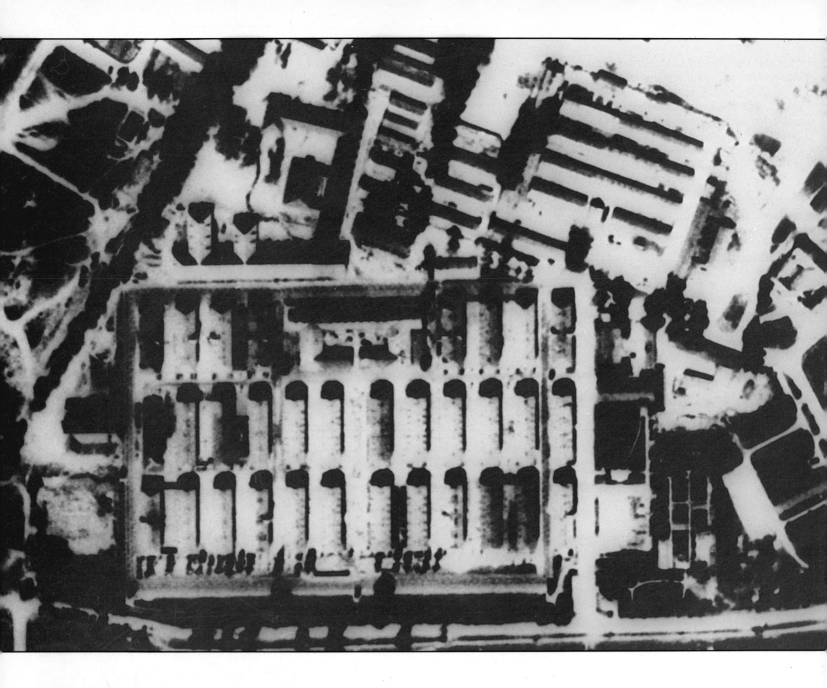

6
Auschwitz I. (Aerial photo taken by the Allies, 25 Aug. 1944; see also map opposite)

7
General plan for Auschwitz I dated 19 February 1942 showing areas intended for the expansion of the camp.

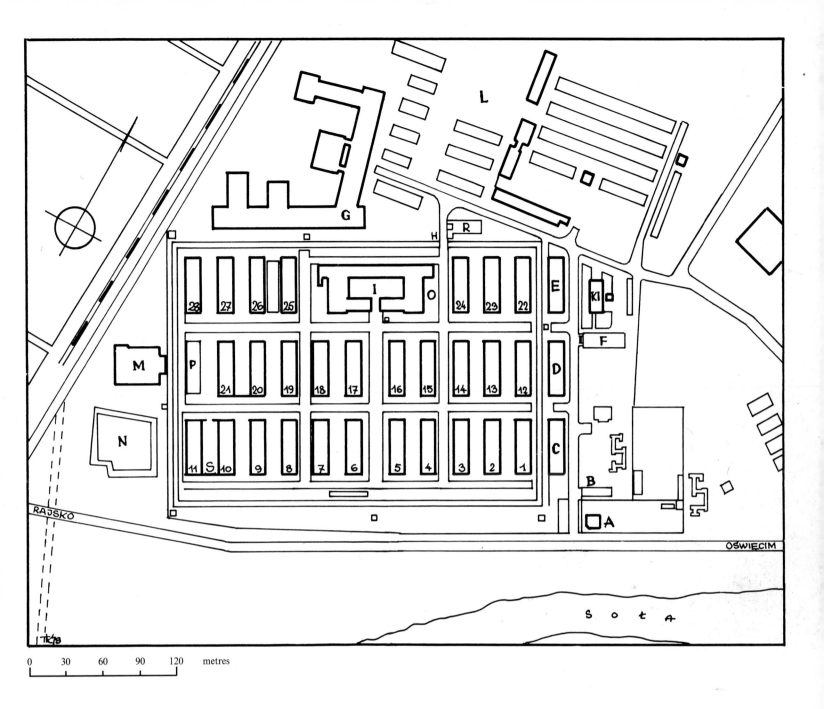

*Map of Auschwitz I
(corresponding to the aerial view
shown in photo 6)*

A House of the camp commandant
B Main guardhouse
C Offices of the camp commandant
D Offices of the camp administration
E Hospital for the SS
F Offices of the Political Section (Gestapo)
G Registration of new prisoners
H Entrance gate with inscription *Arbeit macht frei* ('Work makes you free')
I Kitchen
KI Gas Chamber and Crematorium I

L Stores, stables, garages, and workshops
M Warehouse for belongings taken from deportees and for canisters of the Zyklon B used for mass gassings
N Gravel pit (site of executions)
O Place where the camp orchestra played
P Laundry
R SS guardroom
S Wall where prisoners were executed by shooting

1–28 Blocks housing prisoners

8

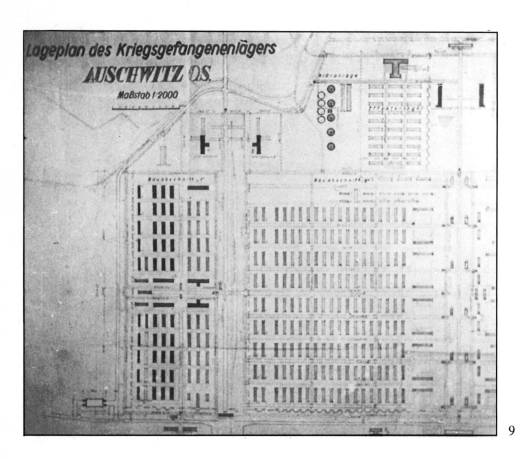

8
Auschwitz II-Birkenau. The majority of the installations used for mass murder were in Auschwitz II-Birkenau. They included four gas chambers, each with its own crematorium, and two improvised gas chambers. Bodies were burned also in pits and adjacent open fields. (Aerial photo taken by the Allies, 21 Dec. 1944; see also map opposite)

9
General plan for Auschwitz II-Birkenau dated 20 March 1943. Note that the camp is described as a *Kriegsgefangenenlager* (camp for prisoners of war).

9

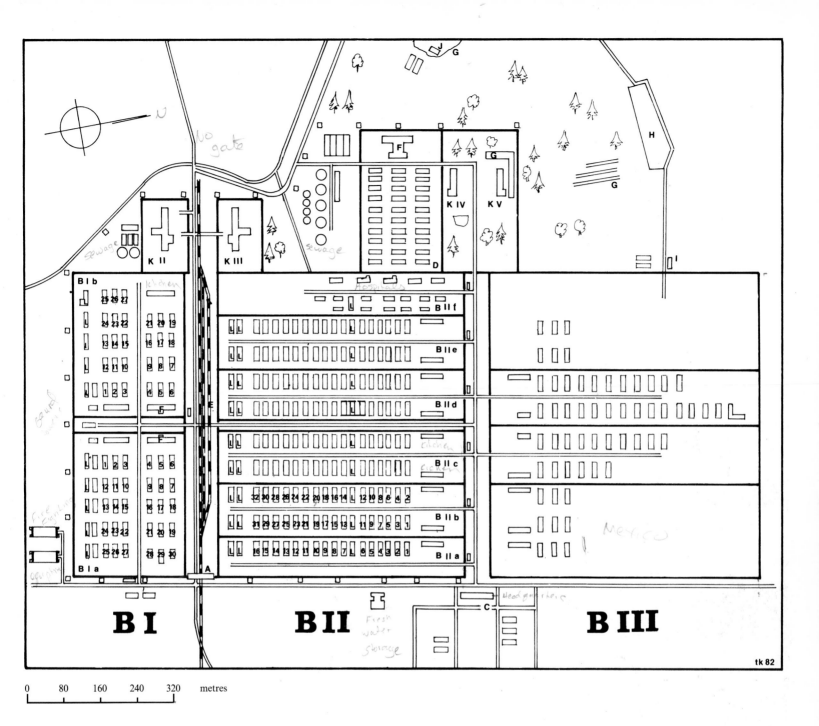

0   80   160   240   320   metres

Map of Auschwitz II-Birkenau (corresponding to the aerial view shown in photo 8)

A   Main gate and guardhouse
BI   Sector I
BII   Sector II
BIII   Sector III ('Mexico'), under construction
BI*a*   Camp for women
BI*b*   Initially a camp for men; from 1943, a camp for women
BII*a*   Quarantine area
BII*b*   Family camp for Jews from Theresienstadt
BII*c*   Camp for Jews from Hungary

BII*d*   Camp for men
BII*e*   Camp for Gypsies
BII*f*   Holding area for sick prisoners ('Infirmary')
C   Camp headquarters and SS barracks
D   'Canada', the area of warehouses used for processing belongings plundered from deportees
E   Ramp where Jews were subjected to selection for the gas chambers as they descended from the trains
F   Showers ('Sauna')
G   Pits and open areas where corpses were burned
H   Mass graves of Soviet prisoners of war

I   First improvised gas chamber (the 'red house')
J   Second improvised gas chamber (the 'white house')
KII   Gas Chamber and Crematorium II
KIII   Gas Chamber and Crematorium III
KIV   Gas Chamber and Crematorium IV
KV   Gas Chamber and Crematorium V
L   Latrines and washrooms

Note: The system of numbering prisoners' barracks in compounds BII*c*, BII*d*, and BII*e* was the same as that in compound BII*b*.

[53]

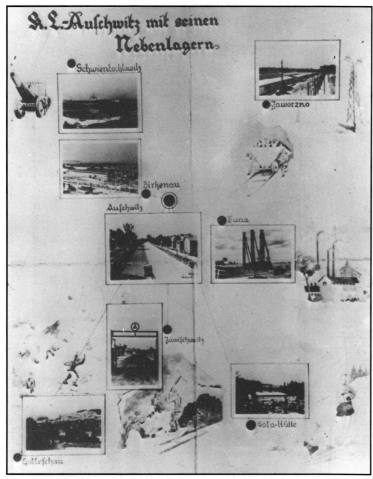

10

Title page of an album made in the camp for the SS. It shows several of the more than forty sub-camps which were set up as part of the Auschwitz complex, mainly at German factories using prisoners for slave labour. (Album prepared by an unknown prisoner, 1943 or 1944)

11

Aerial view of the Auschwitz sub-camp of Łagisza, which was established in September 1943 next to a power plant. (Photo taken by the Allies, 9 July 1944)

10

11

12

Aerial view of Oświęcim-Dwory, where Auschwitz III-Monowitz was set up in 1942 to house slave labour for I. G. Farben's Buna-Werke factory which was to manufacture synthetic oil and rubber for the German army. (Photo taken by the Allies, 29 Nov. 1944)

13

Aerial view of Auschwitz III-Monowitz. (Photo taken by the Allies, 26 June 1944)

12

13

14

Auschwitz I. Main gate with its inscription *Arbeit macht frei* ('Work makes you free'). In fact, prisoners were used as slave labour for ten hours or more each day as a way of deliberately working them to their death. (J. Frąckiewicz, 1960)

15

Auschwitz II-Birkenau. Main guardhouse, which prisoners called the 'Gate of Death', and the railway siding built in 1944 as the last stop for trains carrying Jews. Before that time the trains stopped at an existing goods siding between Auschwitz I and Auschwitz II-Birkenau which was later known as the 'old ramp'. (S. Mucha, 1945)

16

Trzebinia. Main gate leading to the Auschwitz sub-camp of Trzebinia, set up in August 1944 near a German crude-oil refinery. (Photo taken during an inspection after the camp's liberation in 1945)

17

Auschwitz I. Electrified triple barbed-wire fence; its warning sign, in German, reads 'Danger—High Voltage—Lethal'. In the centre is Block 11, called by prisoners the 'Block of Death'. The other side of the wall on the right of this block was where prisoners were executed by shooting. (S. Mucha, 1945)

14

15

16

18

19

18

Auschwitz I. First gas chamber and crematorium (partly reconstructed). The crematorium was brought into operation in 1940, initially to burn the bodies of prisoners who had died from hunger or disease and of those shot or murdered in other ways. At the end of 1941 the Nazis converted its mortuary room into an experimental gas chamber. Its first victims were Soviet prisoners of war and Jews from Silesia who were murdered there with Zyklon B and their bodies then burned. (L. Foryciarz, 1968)

19

Fences at Auschwitz I, viewed from inside the camp. The camp's electrified barbed-wire fences and watch-towers manned by the SS were intended to increase the prisoners' isolation and to make escape impossible. (S. Mucha, 1945)

20

Auschwitz I. The *Blockführerstube,* incorporating the SS guardroom and the office of the camp manager (*Lagerführer*). (S. Łuczko, 1945)

21

Auschwitz II-Birkenau, compound BI*b*. These primitive brick barracks without foundations, the first to be constructed in Auschwitz II-Birkenau, were built by prisoners and Soviet prisoners of war in 1941–2. (S. Kolowca, 1945)

22

Auschwitz II-Birkenau. View of the compound in which a women's camp was established when women were brought from Auschwitz I in August 1942 (BI*a*). In July 1943 the women's camp was expanded to include compound BI*b* too, after the men who had occupied it were transferred to the newly constructed BII*d*. (Photo taken by the SS, 1942 or 1943)

20

21

22

[62]

23

24

25

26

27

23

Auschwitz II-Birkenau. To facilitate control of the tens of thousands of prisoners in Auschwitz II-Birkenau and seal them off more effectively, the various sectors were divided into separate compounds. In this view from the east across sector BII, the separate compounds can be clearly seen. Each compound was surrounded by its own barbed-wire fence—in effect, a camp within a camp. In the foreground are the barracks of BIIa, used from August 1943 for holding new men prisoners in a form of quarantine. Further into the distance can be seen BIIb, used from September 1943 as a camp for Jewish families brought from the ghetto of Theresienstadt; and BIIc, used in 1944 as a camp for Jewish women brought from Hungary. Beyond lay the barracks of BIId, used from July 1943 for men of various nationalities; and of BIIe, used from February 1943 for Gypsies. (Photo taken by the SS, 1943 or 1944)

24

The men's camp of BIId in Auschwitz II-Birkenau. (Photo taken by the SS, 1943 or 1944)

25

Auschwitz II-Birkenau. Gate leading to the road dividing sector BI into compounds BIa and BIb. (H. Makarewicz, 1945)

26

Auschwitz II-Birkenau. Lateral road separating the men's camp (BIId), on the left, from the camp in which Jewish women from Hungary were held in 1944. (Photo taken by the SS, 1943)

27

Auschwitz II-Birkenau. Sector BII, viewed from the west. In the foreground are the wooden barracks of compound BIId, then, consecutively, BIIc, BIIb, and BIIa. (Photo taken from the Soviet film *Chronicle of the Liberation of Auschwitz*, 1945)

28

Auschwitz II-Birkenau. View towards the camp for Gypsies (BII*e*). The marshy soil required the construction of drainage canals. (Photo taken by the SS, winter 1943/4)

29

Auschwitz II-Birkenau. Sector BIII, known by the prisoners as 'Mexico'. Construction started late in 1943 but was discontinued in April 1944. Although 'Mexico' was never finished, more than 10,000 women prisoners, mainly Jews from Hungary, were held there in 1944. (Photo taken by the SS, winter 1943/4)

30

Auschwitz II-Birkenau. Sector BIII under construction. (Photo by the SS, 1944)

28

29

30

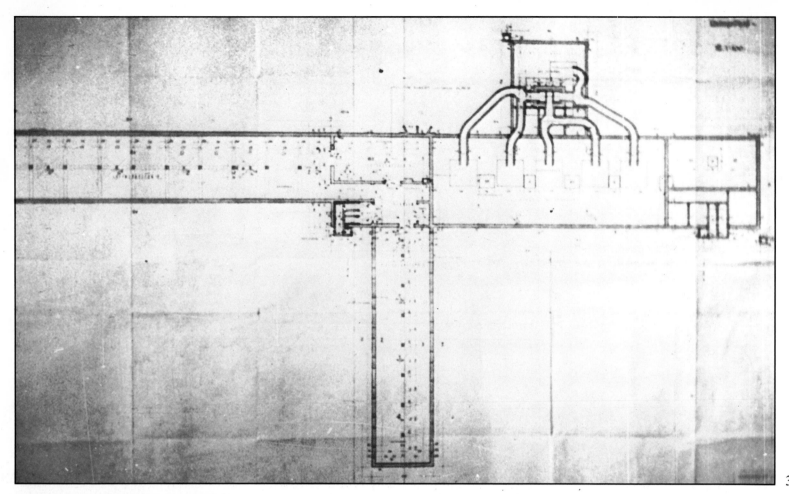

31

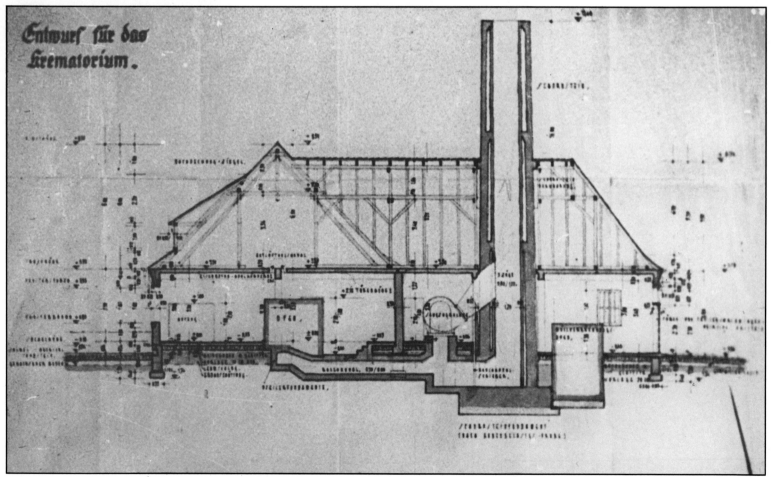

Entwurf für das Krematorium.

32

[66]

31

Plan for a gas chamber and cremat-orium, dated 23 January 1942, that was used for the construction of Gas Chambers and Crematoria II and III. Each of these buildings, called by the Nazis a 'crematorium', in fact comprised an underground hall where victims had to undress (to the left of the plan), a very large underground gas chamber (*c.*210 square metres) where victims were murdered (centre), and five crematorium incinerators for burning their bodies (right).

32

Plan for a gas chamber and cremat-orium, dated 27 January 1942, that was used for the construction of Gas Chambers and Crematoria II and III (vertical section).

33

Auschwitz II-Birkenau. View of Gas Chamber and Crematorium II. The installation was brought into opera-tion on 31 March 1943. The canal in the foreground was an open channel for sewage. (Photo taken by the SS, 1943)

34

Auschwitz II-Birkenau. View of Gas Chamber and Crematorium III. The installation was brought into operation on 25 June 1943. (Photo taken by the SS, 1943)

33

34

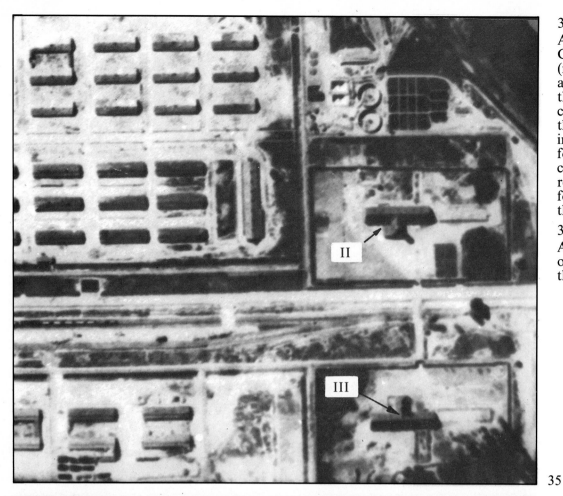

35

Auschwitz II-Birkenau. Gas Chambers and Crematoria II and III (indicated by arrows), seen from the air. In 1944 the SS selection among the new arrivals of deported Jews was carried out on the new railway ramp that ended between these two installations. People considered unfit for work were murdered in the gas chambers, usually the same day; the remainder were taken away for forced labour. (Aerial photo taken by the Allies, 25 Aug. 1944)

36

Auschwitz II-Birkenau. Incinerators of Crematorium II. (Photo taken by the SS, 1943)

35

36

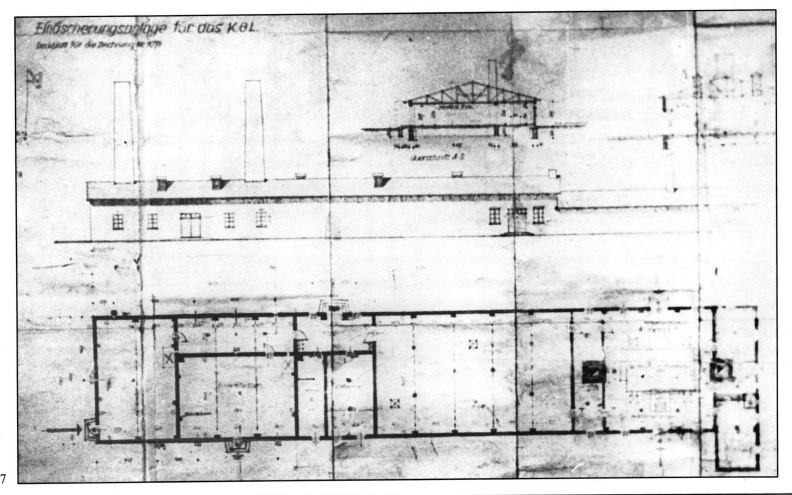

37

37
Plan for a gas chamber and crematorium, dated 11 January 1943, that
was used for Gas Chambers and
Crematoria IV and V. In these two
installations the undressing halls and
gas chambers were on the same level
as the crematorium.

38
Auschwitz II-Birkenau. Gas
Chamber and Crematorium IV. This
installation was brought into
operation on 22 March 1943. (Photo
taken by the SS, 1943)

38

39

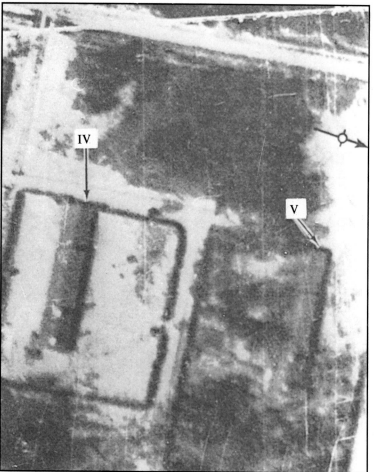

40
41

39

Auschwitz II-Birkenau. Gas Chamber and Crematorium V. This installation was brought into operation on 4 April 1943. (Photo taken by the SS, 1943)

40

Auschwitz II-Birkenau. Gas Chambers and Crematoria IV and V (indicated by arrows), seen from the air. (Photo taken by the Allies, 13 Sept. 1944)

41

Side hatch of a crematorium incinerator, showing the name of the manufacturer, Topf und Söhne. (Photo taken from the Soviet film *Chronicle of the Liberation of Auschwitz*, 1945)

42

Auschwitz II-Birkenau. Part of the brush fence that screened off the area of Gas Chamber and Crematorium V to prevent anyone seeing what was happening there. (S. Kolowca, 1945)

43

Auschwitz II-Birkenau. Warehouses known by the prisoners as 'Canada II'. From December 1943, the clothing, valuables, and other belongings of people who had been murdered were sorted here and then sent elsewhere in the Third Reich for reuse. (Photo taken by the SS, 1943)

42

43

44

45

[72]

44
Barracks in the Trzebinia sub-camp of Auschwitz. (Photo taken during an inspection after the camp's liberation, 1945)

45
Fence around the barracks of the Auschwitz sub-camp set up at Eintrachthütte, the German armaments factory in Świętochłowice, in May 1943. (Photographer and year unknown)

46–7
External and internal views of the crematorium of the Auschwitz sub-camp set up at Blechhammer, the German chemical factory in Blachownia Śląska, in April 1944. It was used to dispose of the bodies of the prisoners who had died there—unlike the crematoria of Auschwitz II-Birkenau, which were used primarily to burn the bodies of people brought specifically to be murdered in the associated gas chambers. (Photographer unknown, photographs taken after the camp's liberation, 1945)

46

47

48

49

[74]

50

48–9
Auschwitz. The camp's several thousand staff were mostly members of the SS-Totenkopfverbände (Death's Head Troops) and were specially trained for service in concentration camps. (Photographers unknown, 1941)

50
Auschwitz. The SS Central Construction Office (*Zentralbauleitung*). (Photo taken by the SS between 1942 and 1944)

51–3
SS-Reichsführer Heinrich Himmler inspecting the construction of I. G. Farben's Buna-Werke factory for synthetic oil and rubber at Oświęcim-Dwory. (Photographers unknown, 1942)

51

52

53

[76]

54

Fritz Bracht, *Gauleiter* (regional party leader) of Silesia (first on the right), on a visit to Auschwitz, accompanied by Rudolf Höss, the camp commandant (centre). (Photographer unknown, photograph taken between 1941 and 1944)

55

Delegation of high-ranking officials of the Third Reich. Such visits were frequent occurrences in Auschwitz. (Photographer unknown, photograph taken between 1940 and 1944)

54

55

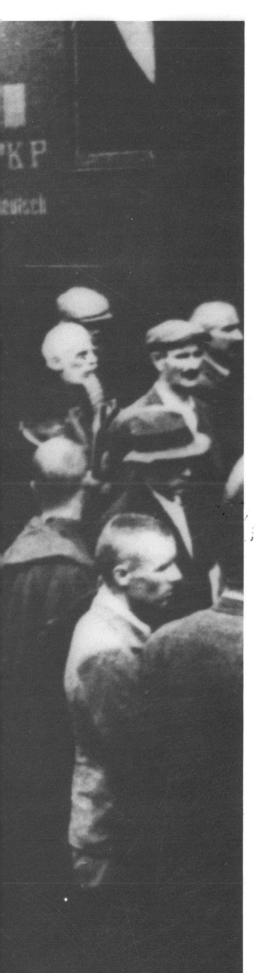

Prisoners held in the concentration camp died from overwork, starvation, sadistic punishments, exhaustion after prolonged roll-calls, torture, appalling sanitary conditions, being used for medical experiments, or arbitrary execution. Those too weak or sick to work were picked out by the SS during roll-calls or in the infirmary and sent to the gas chambers or murdered with phenol injections. Karl Fritzsch, the Schutzhaftlagerführer (camp manager), used to say as much in the speeches he made to prisoners on their arrival: 'This is not a sanatorium,' he would say, 'but a German concentration camp. There is only one exit: through the crematorium chimney. Jews may live for two weeks, priests for one month, the rest for three months.'

56
Tarnów: the first transport being sent to Auschwitz by the Nazis, consisting of 728 Polish political prisoners (including a small number of Jews). At first, Auschwitz was used for Poles: political prisoners, people suspected of being in the resistance movement, intellectuals, and ordinary people arrested during street round-ups. (In total, about 140,000–150,000 Poles were sent to Auschwitz, more than half of whom died there.) It was only later that people of other nationalities (principally Jews) were sent to Auschwitz from all over Europe, making it the largest of the Nazi concentration camps. (Photographer unknown, June 1940)

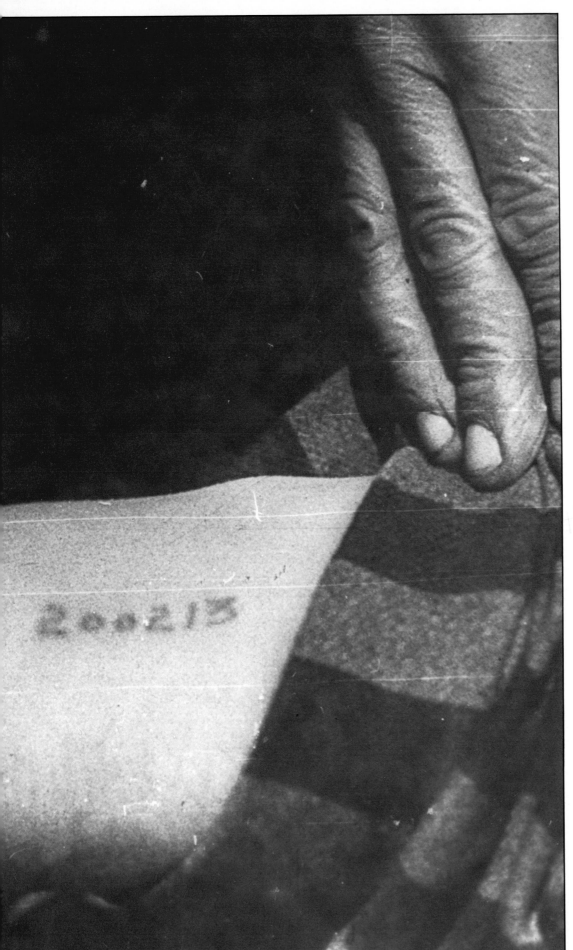

57
For much of the history of the camp, most prisoners were tattooed with a number (a practice used only in Auschwitz). (Photo taken from the Soviet film *Chronicle of the Liberation of Auschwitz,* 1945)

58
Auschwitz II-Birkenau. Interior of the building where new prisoners were registered. It was called 'Sauna' because of the showers that were part of the registration process. Tattooing of prisoners with their numbers was also done here. (Photo taken by the SS, 1944)

59
Auschwitz II-Birkenau. Group of new women prisoners. On arrival prisoners' heads were shaved and they were sent to shower and be deloused and disinfected. Their personal details were then registered and they were given camp clothing and in most cases tattooed with their prison numbers. (Photo taken by the SS, 1944)

57

58

59

60-1

Prisoners' striped clothing allowed them to be picked out at a distance and complicated their hiding in case of escape. On it they had to wear their prison numbers, as well as one or more triangles of coloured cloth indicating the reason for their being in the camp: red for political prisoners, green for professional criminals, black for 'asocials' (Gypsies and also prostitutes), violet for Jehovah's Witnesses, and pink for homosexuals. Jews were given two triangles (in some periods one yellow and one red or green triangle) superimposed to form a Star of David; or sometimes a single yellow triangle together with a red bar to indicate that there was a second reason for their being in the camp; or sometimes a tag with their prisoner number next to a Star of David. (Photo taken from the Soviet film *Chronicle of the Liberation of Auschwitz,* 1945)

62

Auschwitz II-Birkenau. Roll-call of new women prisoners. When the supply of striped clothing ran out, clothes of people who had been gassed on arrival were painted with a coloured stripe or stripes and given to prisoners to wear. (Photo taken by the SS, 1944)

63

The SS ordered the camp orchestra to play marches as prisoners left the camp daily to work, and also when they returned, exhausted and carrying their dead comrades, often eleven or twelve hours later. The thousands of prisoners leaving the camp to work each day were expected to march smartly through the camp's main gate. (Photographer unknown, 1941)

64

Oświęcim town centre. Prisoners demolishing buildings. (Photographer unknown, 1941)

60

61

52

53

65

66

65

Auschwitz II-Birkenau. Prisoners digging a drainage ditch in the camp. (Photo taken by the SS, 1942 or 1943)

66

Auschwitz II-Birkenau. Earthworks going on in the vicinity of Gas Chamber and Crematorium II. In the background, Gas Chamber and Crematorium III under construction. (Photo taken by the SS, winter 1942/3)

67–8

Auschwitz II-Birkenau. Work on the main drainage ditch, known as 'Königsgraben' (literally, 'the king's ditch'). The prisoners engaged in this particularly harsh work were mostly from the special penal unit. (Photos taken by the SS, 1942 or 1943)

67

68

69

70

[88]

69

Auschwitz. Work on the camp's expansion. (Photo taken by the SS, 1942 or 1943)

70

Auschwitz II-Birkenau. Construction of the road to Gas Chambers and Crematoria IV and V. (Photo taken by the SS, 1942)

71

Auschwitz II-Birkenau. Karl Bischoff, the camp's construction manager (second from right), with his assistant, Walter Dejaco, during an inspection of construction work. (Photo taken by the SS, 1942)

72

Auschwitz II-Birkenau. Pouring concrete for Gas Chamber and Crematorium III. (Photo taken by the SS, 1943)

71

72

73

74

73–4
Auschwitz II-Birkenau. Gas
Chamber and Crematorium IV
under construction. (Photos taken by
the SS, winter 1942/3)

75
Auschwitz II-Birkenau. Pouring the
concrete ceiling of the underground
hall of Gas Chamber and Crematorium II where people were to undress
before being murdered. (Photo
taken by the SS, 1943)

75

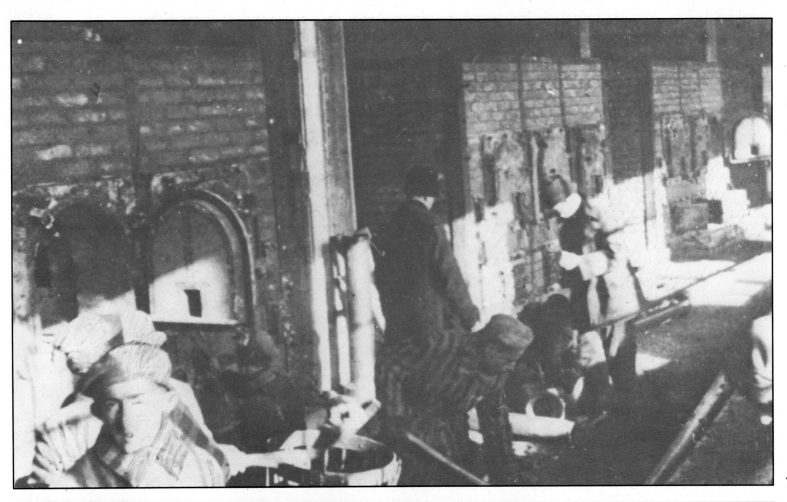

76

77

[92]

76

Auschwitz II-Birkenau. Finishing the inside of Crematorium II. (Photo taken by the SS, 1943)

77

Auschwitz II-Birkenau. Construction of the shower block (the 'Sauna'), brought into use in December 1943. In the background are Gas Chamber and Crematorium IV (right) and Gas Chamber and Crematorium V (among the trees, top left). (Photo taken by the SS, 1943)

78

Auschwitz II-Birkenau. Construction of the sewage plant. There were as many as 90,000 prisoners in Auschwitz II-Birkenau, and the Nazis did not want the rivers polluted with their untreated waste. In the background are the warehouses known by prisoners as 'Canada II' and behind them (centre) the chimneys of Gas Chambers and Crematoria IV and V. (Photo taken by the SS, 1943)

79

Auschwitz II-Birkenau. Construction of the second wing of the main gate and guardhouse. (Photo taken by the SS, winter 1943/4)

78

79

80

81

[94]

80
Auschwitz I. Expansion of the kitchen. (Photo taken by the SS, 1943)

81
Laying the foundations for a new building located in front of Auschwitz I, within the Auschwitz *Interessengebiet*. (Photo taken by the SS, 1942)

82
Constructing the *Schutzhaft-lagererweiterung*—the extension to the base camp—near Auschwitz I. (Photo taken by the SS, 1943)

83
Aerial view of the *Schutzhaft-lagererweiterung*. Its twenty blocks accommodated workshops and some 6,000 women prisoners. (Aerial photo taken by the Allies, 25 Aug. 1944)

82

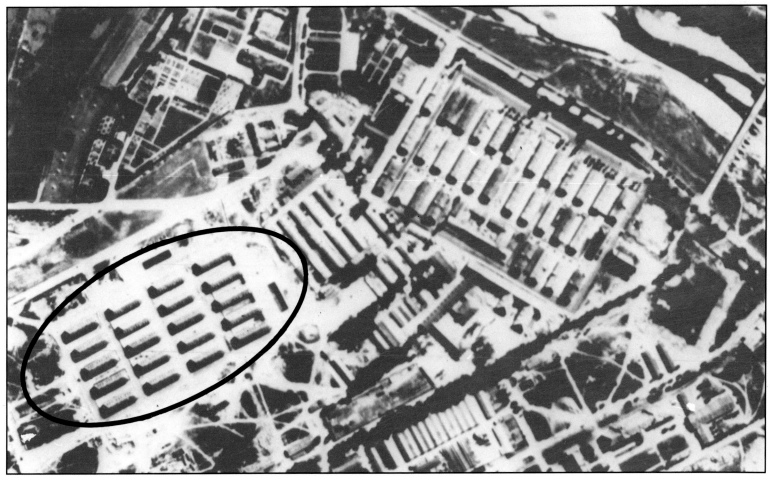

83

84

85

[96]

84
Auschwitz I. Digging trenches to carry hot-water pipes for a proposed central heating system for the offices of the camp administration. In the background is the building where new prisoners were to be registered. (Photo taken by the SS, winter 1943/4)

85
Auschwitz I. The metal-work shop. (Photo taken by the SS, 1942 or 1943)

86
Prisoner employed in the artificial pollination of a rubber plant at the Auschwitz sub-camp of Rajsko. (This description corresponds to the caption originally written on the back of the photo, which is reproduced alongside.) The hands in the photo are those of Wanda Tarasiewicz, a Polish prisoner. The photo was taken by another prisoner, Wanda Jakubowska, in 1944 and smuggled out of the camp.

86

87

87

Oświęcim-Dwory. I. G. Farben's Buna-Werke factory, which was set up to produce synthetic oil and rubber for military use. For this reason it had priority in employing prisoners. (Photo taken from the Soviet film *Chronicle of the Liberation of Auschwitz*, 1945)

88–9

Auschwitz (*Interessengebiet*). Prisoners constructing a factory that was used first by Krupp and later (from 1942) by Union Werke for the production of ammunition. (Photos taken by the SS, 1942 or 1943)

90

Construction of warehouses near Auschwitz II-Birkenau for storing cabbages and potatoes. (Photo taken by the SS, 1943)

91

Finishing the food warehouses. Auschwitz II-Birkenau is in the background, with the main guard-house on the right. (Photo taken by the SS, 1943)

92

Auschwitz I. Transporting food for the prisoners. Standard rations were very small; according to SS calculations, prisoners engaged in forced labour could survive on them for only three to six months. After that time, those who had not died of starvation were suffering from severe malnutrition. (Photo taken by the SS, 1943 or 1944)

'90

91

92

[103]

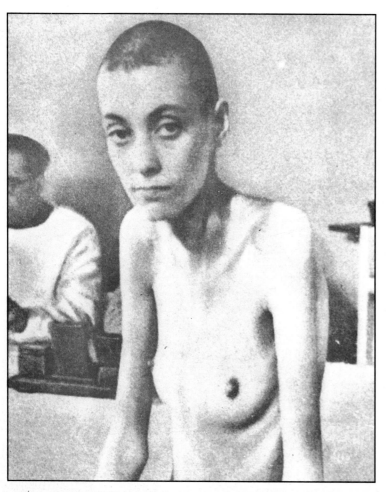
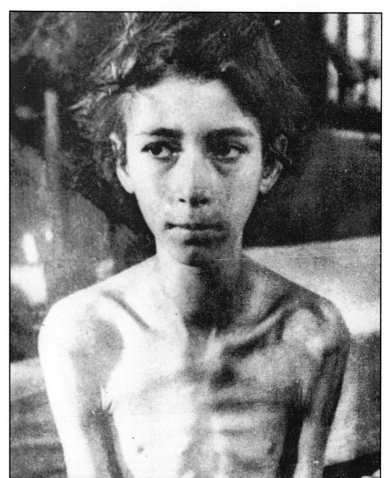

93
94

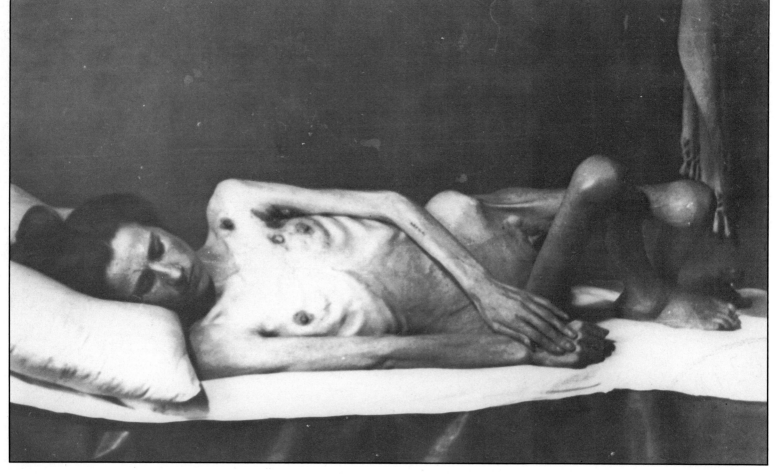

95

[104]

93

A 20-year-old woman from Austria, prisoner number 88972. (Photo taken during a medical examination after the camp's liberation, 1945)

94

A 10-year-old girl from Hungary. (Photo taken during a medical examination after the camp's liberation, 1945)

95

The weight of Polish prisoner 44884 was little more than 55 pounds when the camp was liberated. (Photo taken during a medical examination after the camp's liberation, 1945)

96

A 14-year-old Jewish boy from Hungary, prisoner number B14615. (Photo taken during a medical examination after the camp's liberation, 1945)

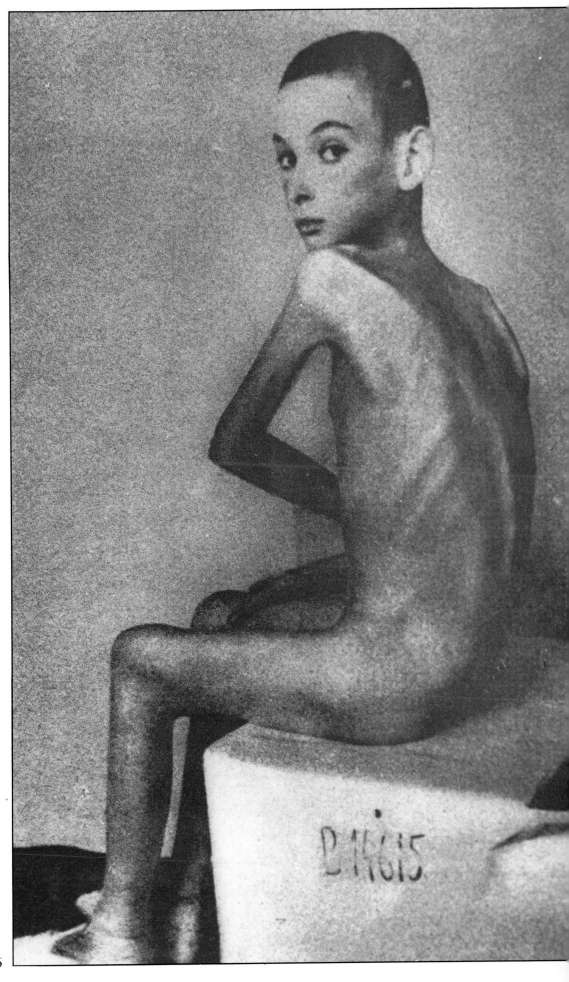

96

97

98

[106]

97
Marshy conditions in the camp accelerated the spread of diseases, including malaria. (Photo taken by the SS, 1942 or 1943)

98
Auschwitz II-Birkenau. Hundreds of prisoners were crowded into barracks originally designed as stables for fifty-two horses. (Photo taken from the Soviet film *Chronicle of the Liberation of Auschwitz*, 1945)

99
Auschwitz I. As the prisoner population of Auschwitz grew, more and more prisoners were held in each barrack. Originally they slept on the floor, on straw or later on straw mattresses; more than 1,000 persons were crowded into a single barrack. Later on, three-tier plank beds were introduced, and prisoners were also held in cellars and garrets. (S. Mucha, 1945)

100
Primitive latrines in Auschwitz II-Birkenau. Prisoners had access to latrines for only a few minutes before leaving for work in the early morning and after coming back from work in the evening. (Photo taken by the SS, 1943 or 1944)

99

100

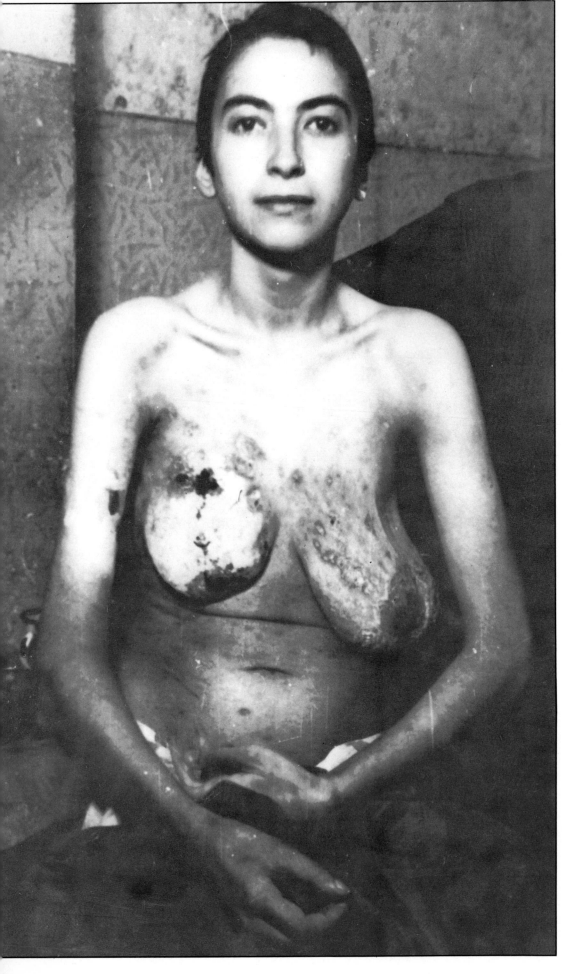

A Jewish woman from Hungary, prisoner number A11380, photographed during a medical examination after the camp's liberation. Her condition was not unusual. Horrific hygienic and sanitary conditions accelerated the spread of typhus, prurigo, and phlegmons. (S. Łuczko, 1945)

101

102

Auschwitz I. The sign above the entrance to Block 21, used as an infirmary for prisoners, read (in German) 'Surgical Department'. Among prisoners it was known as the 'crematorium waiting-room', because SS doctors conducted medical experiments on the prisoners there and murdered the sick and weak by injecting phenol to the heart. Similar 'infirmaries' were to be found in all camps, including Auschwitz II-Birkenau (compound BII*f*) and Auschwitz III-Monowitz. Medical facilities were virtually non-existent there; rather, they served for the isolation of sick prisoners who would subsequently often be murdered. (Photo taken after the camp's liberation, 1945)

103

A hypodermic syringe used by the SS to murder prisoners by administering phenol.

104

Drugs made by I. G. Farben (Bayer) were tested on prisoners by the SS.

105

Auschwitz II-Birkenau. (A. Bujak, 1970)

102

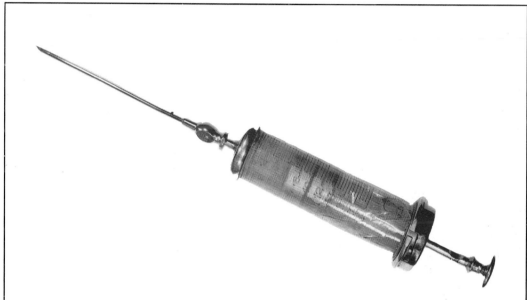

103

104

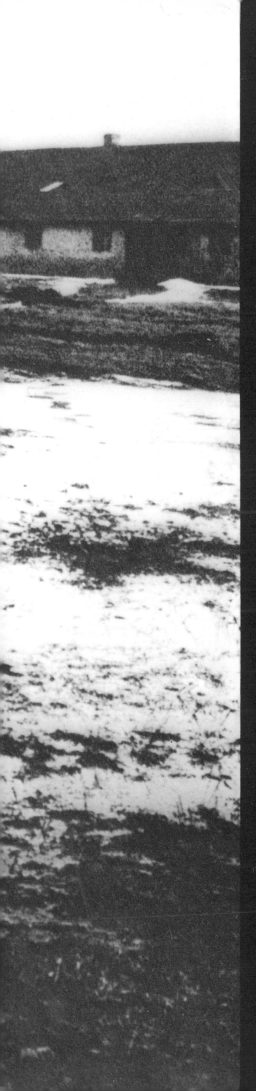

Conditions in Birkenau were much worse than in Auschwitz. At each step, one's feet would get stuck in the mud. There was virtually no water for washing. Prisoners slept on three-tier plank beds, six prisoners to a bed. The majority of plank beds did not have even straw mattresses. During the twice-daily roll-calls, prisoners were forced to stand for many hours in cold weather, their feet deep in the mud; when it rained, they had to sleep in their wet clothing. Hundreds of prisoners died every day. Because of the barbaric hygienic conditions, insufficient food, hard work, and other torments, the majority of the prisoners died miserable deaths within several weeks, or at the most several months. Even women, dressed in rags or in Russian army coats, had to do heavy work, moving stones or digging. Only those prisoners who managed to get a special post or work in one of the few work units where conditions were better were able to stay alive a little longer. Auschwitz was an extermination camp, the largest that ever existed.

Pery Broad

106–7
Professor Carl Clauberg (photo 106) conducted experiments on Jewish women in Block 10 of Auschwitz I (photo 107) to devise a rapid method for mass sterilization. The intention was to use it for the biological genocide of the Slavs. (Photographers and year unknown)

10

108–9
Auschwitz I. Interior of Block 10.
Wooden screens were placed on the
windows so that the women inside
would not be able to see the
executions that took place in the yard
between Blocks 10 and 11. In fact,
however, they were able to see
through cracks in the wood. (Photo
108: Ž. Łoboda, 1968; photo 109:
photographer and year unknown)

108

09

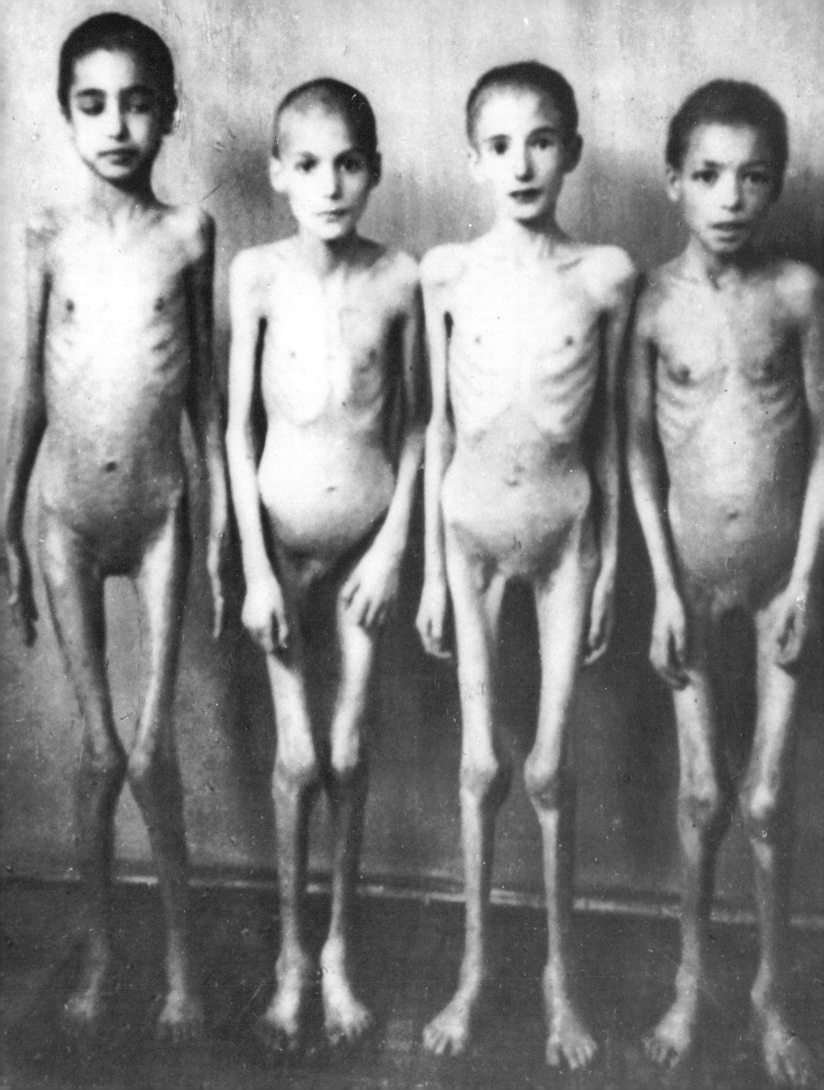

110–12

Dr Joseph Mengele (photo 112) conducted experiments to test aspects of heredity. His experiments were conducted on twins (photo 110), dwarves (photo 111), and people crippled from birth. (Photo 110: from Dr Mengele's personal files; photo 111: taken by the SS, 1944; photo 112: photographer and year unknown)

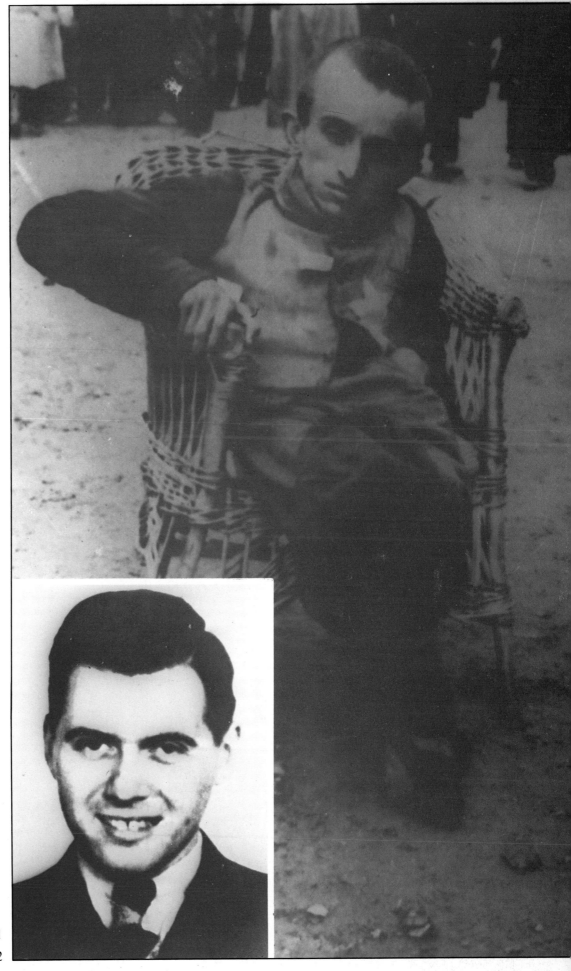

111

112

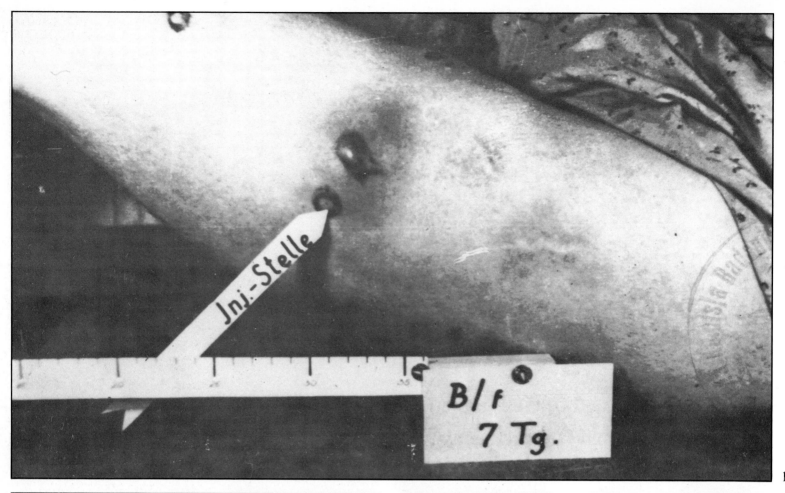

Jnj.-Stelle

B/f
7 Tg.

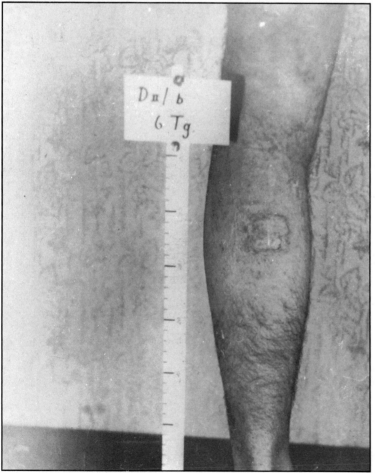

Dп/b
6 Tg.

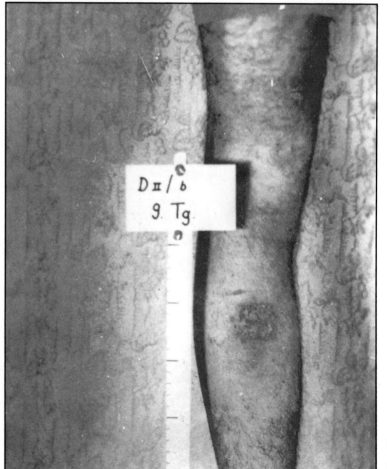

Dп/b
9 Tg.

[116]

113–15

On the instructions of the Wehrmacht, healthy prisoners were used as guinea-pigs for testing toxic substances. The experiments were conducted by Emil Kaschub, a German doctor. They involved applying these substances to the hands and legs, causing festering and painful wounds. (E. Kaschub, 1944)

116

Auschwitz II-Birkenau. Interior of a barrack used to house a special penal unit from May 1942 to July 1943. On the ceiling is a drawing made by prisoners of this unit, showing their suffering in excavating 'Königsgraben', the main drainage ditch of Auschwitz II-Birkenau (see also photos 67–8). (T. Kinowski, 1954)

116

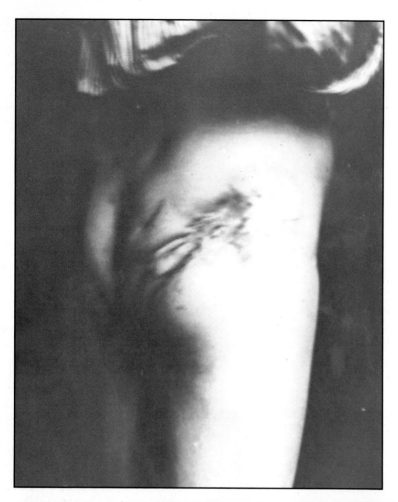

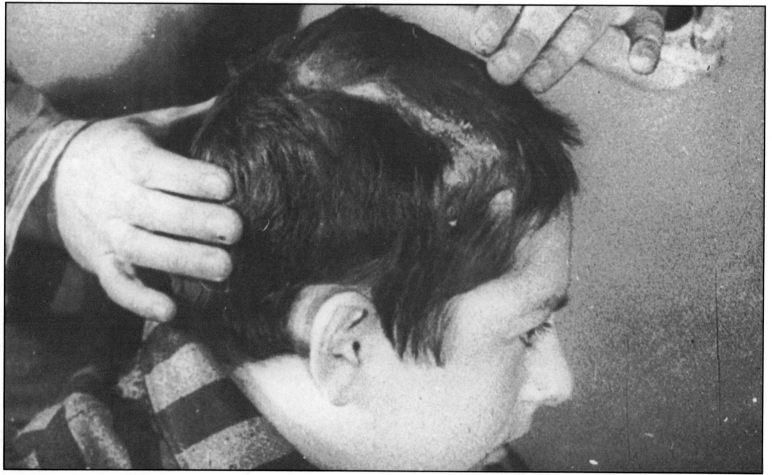

117
Whippings caused serious and lasting injuries. (Photo taken during a medical inspection after the camp's liberation, 1945)

118
Bench on which prisoners were whipped. The official maximum punishment was supposed to be twenty-five lashes, but prisoners sometimes received as many as seventy. (S. Kolowca, 1945)

119
This Hungarian boy received injuries to his skull when an SS officer struck him for giving his bread to a starving woman prisoner. (Photo taken from the Soviet film *Chronicle of the Liberation of Auschwitz*, 1945)

120–1
Frostbite, caused by standing to attention for long periods in the freezing Auschwitz winters (a favourite SS punishment), or by working outdoors without adequate protection, often led to the onset of gangrene and a painful death. (Photos taken from the Soviet film *Chronicle of the Liberation of Auschwitz*, 1945)

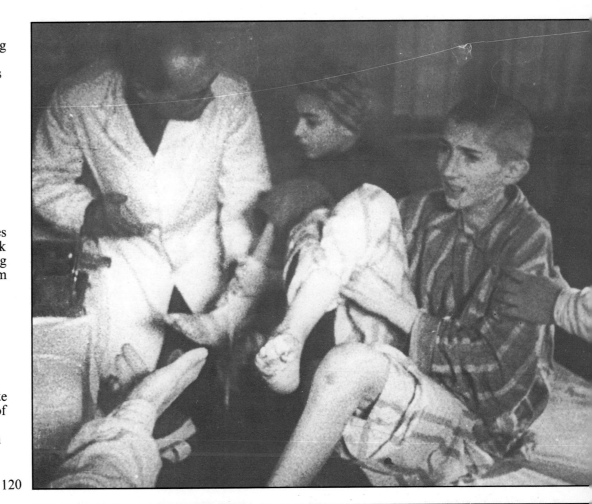

120

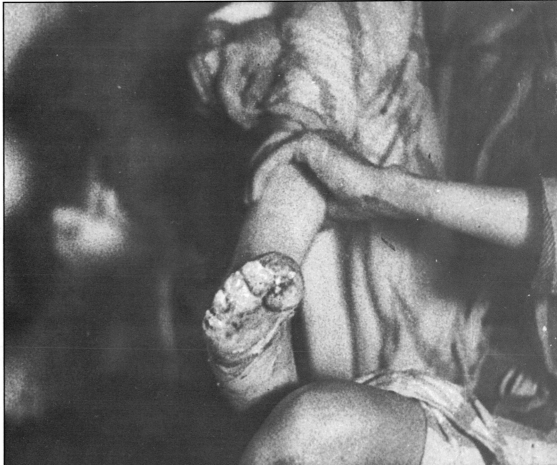

121

[119]

122

123

[120]

122

Auschwitz I. Block 11, known by prisoners as the 'Block of Death'. (L. Foryciarz, 1968)

123

Block 11 in Auschwitz I: entrance to the 'standing cells'. Up to four prisoners at a time were held in these 36 x 36-in. cells in punitive overnight detention. Prisoners had to crawl in through these kennel-like entrances. (T. Kinowski, 1954)

124

Cellars of Block 11 where prisoners under interrogation were tortured. In September 1941, 600 Soviet prisoners of war and 250 Polish political prisoners were taken from the camp infirmary and murdered here with Zyklon B gas to test its efficiency as an instrument of mass murder. (T. Kinowski, 1954)

124

125

Starvation cell in the cellars of Block 11. Ten to twenty prisoners would be held in such cells to die of starvation as a collective punishment for the escape of a single prisoner. One of the groups of prisoners condemned to die in this way in 1941 included Father Maksymilian Kolbe, a Polish Franciscan who volunteered his own life in place of that of another Polish prisoner. Maksymilian Kolbe was subsequently canonized;
(T. Kinowski, 1954)

126

To prevent prisoners confined in the standing cells of Block 11 having contact with other prisoners, the inlets for ventilation were only 2 inches square—and even these small openings were covered with perforated metal screens. In winter, if frozen snow blocked the perforations, prisoners sometimes died of suffocation. (T. Kinowski, 1954)

127

Auschwitz I. Portable gallows used to hang prisoners caught trying to escape or suspected of participation in the resistance movement. The picture was taken in the yard of Block 11 and shows representatives of the Soviet Commission for the Investigation of Nazi Crimes (left) and liberated prisoners. (Photo taken from the Soviet film *Chronicle of the Liberation of Auschwitz*, 1945)

125

6

27

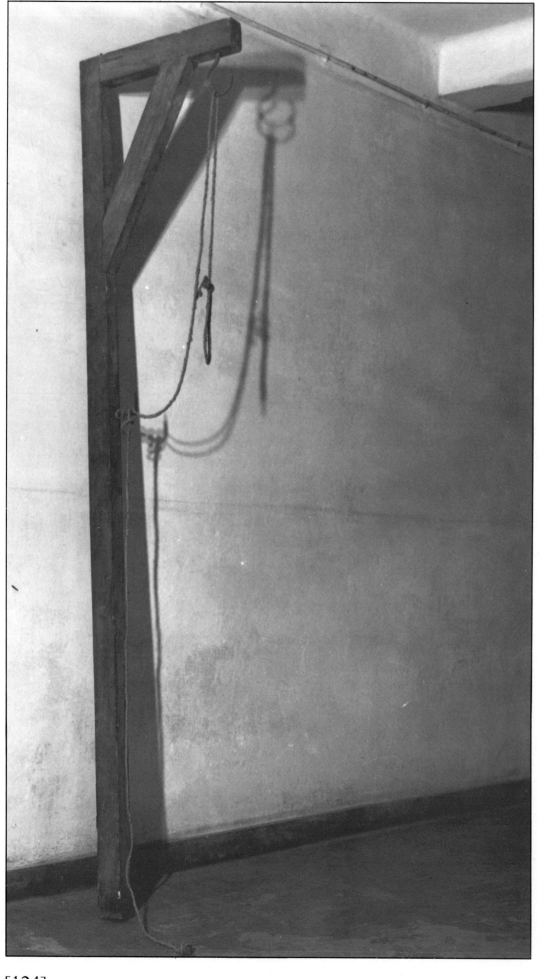

128
Auschwitz I. Punishments imposed on prisoners included having their arms twisted behind their backs and then being suspended by their wrists from posts like these for hours on end. (L. Foryciarz, 1968)

129
Auschwitz I. A collective gallows (reconstructed). Twelve Polish political prisoners were hanged on a gallows here on 19 July 1943 because they were suspected of having helped three people escape and of contacting Poles living in the vicinity of the camp. (T. Kinowski, 1954)

130
Auschwitz I. Several thousand prisoners were shot against this wall. For the most part these were Poles —either members of the resistance movement or people sentenced to death by the visiting Nazi tribunal from the nearby town of Katowice. The black wall was reconstructed by the Museum. (T. Kinowski, 1954)

29

30

SS-Hauptsturmführer Aumeier took the opportunity to show his unprecedented brutality when thirteen Polish engineers[1] were hanged publicly 'in retaliation' for the attempted escape by a prisoner[2] from a work detail of the Zentralbauleitung. They were executed on the square in front of the kitchen, in the presence of other prisoners standing at roll-call. An iron rail was placed on two posts. The ropes from which the prisoners were hanged proved to be too short: a fall from that height could not cause the neck vertebrae to break . . . The stools were removed from under the victims' feet. The bodies continued to writhe convulsively for several minutes. Aumeier said, 'Let them writhe for a while,' but then he lost patience and gave the execution squad the order: 'Jump on them!' The prisoners standing nearby clenched their fists. The torments of the victims sentenced 'in retaliation' brought tears to the eyes of the prisoners witnessing the execution.

Pery Broad

[1] In fact, twelve engineers; see Caption 129.
[2] In fact, three prisoners; see Caption 129.

A black wall was constructed in front of the brick wall in the yard of Block 11. That wall, with its covering of black [cork] insulating plates, marked the final milestone of thousands of innocent people: patriots who did not want to betray their homeland for financial benefit, prisoners who had managed to escape from Auschwitz but had had the bitter misfortune to be caught, people from all the countries occupied by the Germans—all were executed at the 'black wall'. The shootings were done by a Rapportführer or by a guard. So as not to attract the attention of people on the main road beyond the other side of the wall, the weapon used would be a small-calibre rifle with a magazine for ten or fifteen cartridges. Several terrified grave-diggers stood by, stretchers at the ready, to carry out their grim duty, unable to hide the horror on their faces. Another prisoner, one of the men who used to clean the block and was particularly strong, brought the first two victims at the double. He kept hold of their arms and pressed their faces to the wall. 'Preste!' (Straight!) was the command if they turned their heads aside. Though they were walking skeletons (many of them having spent months in stinking cells in conditions unsuitable even for animals) and could hardly stand upright, many of them shouted at the final moment, 'Long live Poland!', or 'Long live freedom!' When this happened an orderly would shoot them quickly in the back of the head or try to silence them with brutal blows.

This was how Poles and Jews would die. Nazi propaganda repeated over and over again that the prisoners were slave skunks whining for mercy and that they had no right at all to live. Only Germans had that right.

Pery Broad

131
The last letters of some Poles
sentenced to be shot. The letters were
smuggled out to their families.

Translation of letter above

Dear Stephanie my wife,
  Today on 31st October I will die
without being guilty. Remember me
always, my wife. Bring up our
beloved little daughter properly. May
Jesus take care of her. When you get
this card, show it to my mother.
  My dear Mother and brothers and
sisters, live in harmony, and do not
do any harm to my little daughter
and my wife. God be with you. Pray
for me.

Translation of letter above

Dear finder,

My dearest friend, read this and be so kind as to mail this. Be so good. Let it reach my family.

Translation of letter in centre of page

Farewell, my most beloved wife, my dearest Lolunia, and my mother. I am about to leave this world. I am going to be sent to the ovens on the 30th at 7 o'clock in the evening. I have been sentenced to death as a bandit.

My dearest Bronisława, I am sorry to leave you. Believe me, I cannot write more, because my hand is trembling and my eyes are full of tears because I die so consciously and without being guilty.

Fifty-eight of us will die, including ten women. I kiss you and Lolunia many times. At 7 o'clock in the evening . . . I think of you. On the 30th of October, pray, say your prayers. Tell Lolunia that father has already passed away. I cannot write. I cannot write. Farewell, all of you. Be with God.

132
Auschwitz II-Birkenau. Cart-load of
bodies. (Photographer unknown,
1945)

The Führer has ordered the final solution of the Jewish question, and we, the SS, are to carry out this order. The extermination centres already existing in the east are not in a position to carry out the operation on the large scale planned. I have therefore selected Auschwitz for this purpose: it is situated conveniently from the point of view of transportation and it will be easy to seal off and camouflage the designated area . . . You will keep this order absolutely confidential, even from your superiors. After your talk with Eichmann you should immediately send me the plans for the projected installations. The Jews are age-old enemies of the German people and must be eliminated. All Jews whom we can lay hands on during this war will be put to death, without exception.

SS-Reichsführer Heinrich Himmler, as reported by Rudolf Höss in his autobiography

133

Auschwitz II-Birkenau. More than a million Jews from almost all over Europe were deported to Auschwitz. The intention of the Nazis was to murder them all, without exception. However, those Jews whom they considered strong and healthy enough to work were selected from among the mass of Jews arriving on the transports. It was not that they were to be reprieved from the death sentence, but rather that they should contribute their labour to the German war effort until they dropped dead from exhaustion, starvation, or disease.

The SS used prisoners to assist with the arrivals. Their job was to help keep them calm, to take away the baggage, to unload any dead bodies, and in general to clear the area (or 'ramp', as it was called) so that people arriving on the next transport would have no idea what was awaiting them when they disembarked from the train.

This photograph shows the arrival of a transport of Jews from Hungary. A prisoner, in striped clothing, can be clearly seen in the foreground. The building in the background with the chimney housed Gas Chamber and Crematorium II. (Photo taken by the SS, 1944)

134

Most Jews who were sent to Auschwitz from 1942 onwards were deceived by the Nazis into thinking that they were being taken to a place where they would be able to live and work in peace, but in fact they were being taken to be murdered.

In March 1943, the Nazis started deporting Jews from Greece to Auschwitz by the train-load. The railway tickets from Greece had to be paid for, none the less; sometimes the SS paid and were reimbursed from Germany, sometimes the Jewish community paid, and sometimes the individual Jews themselves paid for the ticket that would take them to their death. When Auschwitz was liberated, about 30,000 railway tickets, printed in German and Greek, were discovered near where they had got off the train. (L. Foryciarz, 1968)

134

135

Auschwitz II-Birkenau. From left to right in a clockwise direction, the arrows show: a column of people adjacent to a stationary train; Gas Chamber and Crematorium II; the gate to the compound containing Gas Chamber and Crematorium II; and Gas Chamber and Crematorium III. (Aerial photo taken by the Allies, 25 Aug. 1944)

136, 138–46

Auschwitz II-Birkenau. Arrival of Jews from Hungary. Many of the Jews deported to Auschwitz from Hungary were not in fact Hungarian but came from those parts of Slovakia and Transylvania that had been annexed by Hungary earlier in the war. (Photos taken by the SS, 1944)

137

Arrival of a transport of Jews inside Auschwitz II-Birkenau. To the top left of the photograph one can see the main guardhouse and watch-tower; through them ran the railway line that led to Gas Chambers and Crematoria II and III. (Photo taken by the SS, 1944)

135

6

7

13.

14.

A long line of sealed freight cars stood in a siding. The doors of the cars were fastened with wire. Floodlights shone down on the train and the unloading ramp alongside. Worried faces could be seen peering through the barbed wire that criss-crossed the small openings. The guards were in position around the train and on the ramp. Their commander reported to the SS man responsible for receiving the transport that all his men were in position. The cars could be unloaded. The commander of the escort squad that had guarded the train on its journey . . . handed over the details of the transport to an SS man of the receiving squad. The list contained the name of the place that the transport had come from, the number of the train, and the names, surnames, and dates of birth of the Jews brought to Auschwitz. The SS of the camp garrison had meanwhile got the new arrivals off the train. Complete chaos ensued on the ramp.

Pery Broad

141

142

[139]

The mass is divided into three groups: women and children; boys and old men; and the third group, the smallest, about 10 per cent of the transport. No one knows which group is better, safer. Everyone guesses that this is a selection for different kinds of work. Women and children for very light work, boys and old men for ordinary work. The third, the smallest group, with the ones who look fittest, must be destined for very hard work.

        Zalmen Gradowski

143

[140]

144

145

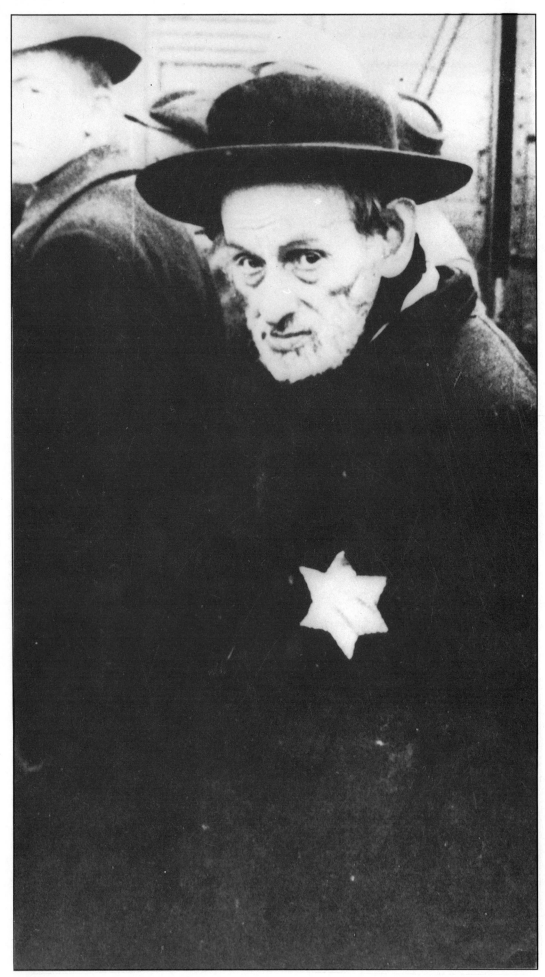

First the men and the women are divided. Heartbreaking scenes of farewell. Husbands and wives are separated, mothers wave to their sons for the last time.

The lines of prisoners stand on the platform in ranks of five, several metres apart. If someone succumbs to the pain of separation and runs up to the other line again, to give his hand to one he loves, to whisper a few consoling words, a sharp blow from an SS man sends him staggering back. Now the SS doctor begins to segregate those who are fit for work, in his opinion, from those who are not. As a rule, mothers with little children are classed as not fit for work, as are those who look weak or sick. Wooden steps are brought to the back of the truck, and the ones the doctor selected as unfit for work have to get in. The SS men from the receiving unit count off everyone climbing the steps. Likewise they count all the ones fit for work, who have to start marching to the men's or women's camp. All the baggage must remain on the platform. The captives are told it will be taken later by truck. That is true, too, but none of the prisoners will ever see their property again.

Pery Broad

147–51
Auschwitz II-Birkenau. Immediately on disembarking from the train, the Jews were ordered into two columns, one of women and children and the other of men. Each column was subjected to selection by SS doctors and medical orderlies, there and then on the ramp: the strong and healthy were separated from the old, the sick, and children. People selected as fit for work were sent for forced labour. The others, usually 70 to 75 per cent of a transport, were sent to be murdered in the gas chambers. (Photos taken by the SS, 1944)

146

147

48

149

150

[144]

*We are in the death camp. It is
a lifeless island. A man does not come
here to live but to die, sooner or later.
There is no room for life here. It is the
residence of death. Our brains are
dulled, thoughts are numbed, this new
language is impossible to grasp.
Everyone is wondering where his
family is. Where were they taken and
how will they manage in the new
conditions? Who knows how their
terrified children will behave when
they see how their mothers are
mistreated? Who knows how these
thugs will treat the sick, the weakened
mothers, and the sisters they love?
Who knows what human grave
received their fathers and brothers, or
what they are going through? They all
stand helpless, full of anxiety, in
despair, lonely, wretched, broken.*

Zalmen Gradowski

151

152

152
Auschwitz II-Birkenau. After
a selection. The column of people
seen here are Jews being led away to
the gas chambers, having been
selected for immediate death. Their
route takes them past the barrack
used as the *Blockführerstube* and on
to the main road of the camp, which
led directly to Gas Chambers and
Crematoria II and III. To prevent
panic among the victims, the SS told
them that they were being taken to
the showers—and indeed the gas
chambers were fitted out inside to
resemble shower-rooms. (Photo
taken by the SS, 1944)

[145]

153

154

[146]

153–4

Auschwitz II-Birkenau. Jewish mothers with children and older women on their way to the gas chambers. In the background of photo 154 is Gas Chamber and Crematorium III. (Photos taken by the SS, 1944)

155–7

Auschwitz II-Birkenau. Jewish women and children on the way to their deaths in Gas Chamber IV or V. All these photos were taken on the road between compounds BII*c* and BII*d*. In photos 156 and 157, the freight wagons on which they had arrived can be seen in the background. (Photos taken by the SS, 1944)

155

156

[147]

157

158

[148]

9

158–9 *and next page*
Auschwitz II-Birkenau. Jews waiting their turn for the gas chambers. (Photos taken by the SS, 1944)

160
Auschwitz II-Birkenau. The last moments before death. The building housing Gas Chamber and Crematorium IV is in the background. (Photo taken by the SS, 1944)

160

[149]

16

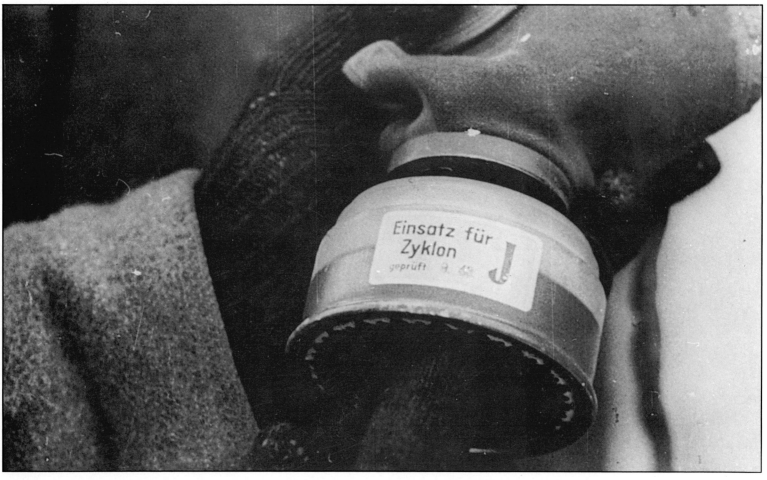

16

161
False showerheads like these were mounted in the ceilings of the gas chambers in Auschwitz II-Birkenau.

162
Part of a protective mask used by the SS when gassing people. (Photo taken from the Soviet film *Chronicle of the Liberation of Auschwitz*, 1945)

163
The SS monitored the progress of the gassing through peep-holes such as this. (Photo taken from the Soviet film *Chronicle of the Liberation of Auschwitz*, 1945)

164–5
Canisters of the Zyklon B used for mass murder in Auschwitz. Supplied in the form of pellets of diatomite saturated with hydrogen cyanide, it gave off a poisonous gas when brought into contact with air. The substance was manufactured by Degesch (Deutsche Gesellschaft für Schädlingsbekämpfung), a Hamburg pest control firm, as a regular pesticide: the mass murders were in effect conceived by the Nazis as a sanitary operation designed to exterminate human beings they classified as vermin. (Photo 164: taken from the Soviet film *Chronicle of the Liberation of Auschwitz*, 1945)

163

164

165
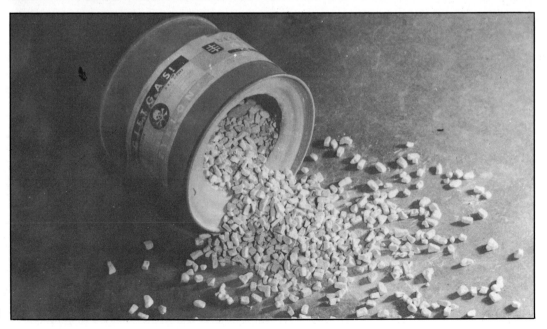

Those Jews selected for extermination were brought as quietly as possible, men and women separately, to the [buildings housing the gas chambers and] crematoria. In the undressing room, the Sonderkommando prisoners who worked there would tell them in their native language that they were now going for a shower and delousing. They were instructed to fold their clothes tidily and to make sure they remembered precisely where they had left them so that they would be able to find them quickly again afterwards. . . .

After undressing, the Jews were sent into the gas chamber: it had shower installations and water pipes so that it would look just like a shower room, but in fact it was a gas chamber. The women and children were sent in first, then the men, always fewer in number. . . .

The levers locking the door were then quickly shut tight. Fumigators[1] who were on stand-by outside then immediately emptied the Zyklon B down through special shafts that opened into outlets in the ceiling. . . . Through a peep-hole in the door one could see that the people standing nearest the outlets dropped dead immediately. . . .

Half an hour after the gas had been introduced, the door was opened, the ventilation system was switched on, and removal of the corpses began right away. . . . The Sonderkommando extracted any gold teeth, cut off the women's hair, and then loaded the corpses on to lifts to take them up to the incinerators, which had been stoked up in advance. Depending on the size of the corpses, up to three could be put into an incinerator at the same time.

Rudolf Höss

---

[1] Höss's term for the murderers.

166

Interior of the gas chamber of Auschwitz I. This gas chamber, the first to be used in Auschwitz, operated from the end of 1941 to 1942. It was not originally constructed as a gas chamber, having been improvised in the mortuary of the camp's crematorium.

Early in 1942, two small improvised gas chambers were brought also into operation in Auschwitz II-Birkenau —the 'red house' and the 'white house'. They were the first sites of gassings in that camp and were in use for about a year; the white house was also reopened in 1944, as an additional gas chamber that was brought back into service during the mass murder of the Jews from Hungary. (A. Kaczkowski, 1970)

167

Auschwitz I. An incinerator installation in Crematorium I. The trolleys in front of the incinerators were used for transporting the bodies from gas chamber and loading them into the incinerators; the metal device on the floor is part of a switching facility that enabled the trolleys to be rotated through 90°.

In 1943, when the gas chambers and crematoria of Auschwitz II-Birkenau were brought into operation, this crematorium was closed down. The incinerators were dismantled and the building was used as an air-raid shelter instead. After the war the crematorium installation was reconstructed as part of the Museum, using original metal components found in the camp. (L. Foryciarz, 1968)

168

Auschwitz II-Birkenau. Incinerators in a crematorium. (Photo taken by the SS, 1943)

169

Auschwitz II-Birkenau. Human remains still evident in an incinerator in Crematorium V destroyed by the SS prior to evacuating the camp. (Photo taken from the Soviet film *Chronicle of the Liberation of Auschwitz*, 1945)

167

68

59

17

17

[160]

Only towards the end of the summer of 1942, did we begin to dispose of bodies by burning them: at first 2,000 at a time on pyres of wood; later in pits, together with bodies that had previously been buried. Crude oil wastes and later methanol were poured over them; the bodies were burned in the pits continuously, that is, day and night.

Rudolf Höss

173

174

170–3

Auschwitz II-Birkenau. Charred human remains found lying on the ground when the camp was liberated. In spite of working round the clock, the incinerators could not cope with the number of bodies that were to be incinerated, so bodies were also burned in the open air. (Photo 170: taken from the Soviet film *Chronicle of the Liberation of Auschwitz*, 1945; photo 171: H. Makarewicz, 1945; photo 172: taken after the camp's liberation; photo 173: photographer unknown)

174

Auschwitz II-Birkenau. One of the pits in which bodies were burned. (Z. Łoboda, 1968)

[161]

175

The Nazis exploited even the corpses of their victims for economic benefits. Gold and other precious metals were removed from the teeth of those who had been murdered, melted down into bars, and sent to the SS Main Sanitary Office (SS-Sanitätshauptamt). Sets of false teeth such as those in the picture were also removed for reuse. Whole skeletons were sold for teaching purposes in medical research institutes. (Photo taken during an inspection after the camp's liberation, 1945)

176–7

Hair of women murdered in Auschwitz was sold to German firms such as Alex Zink for 50 pfennigs a kilogramme. (Photo taken from the Soviet film *Chronicle of the Liberation of Auschwitz*, 1945)

178

Cloth made of human hair. (Photo taken after the camp's liberation, 1945)

175

176

[162]

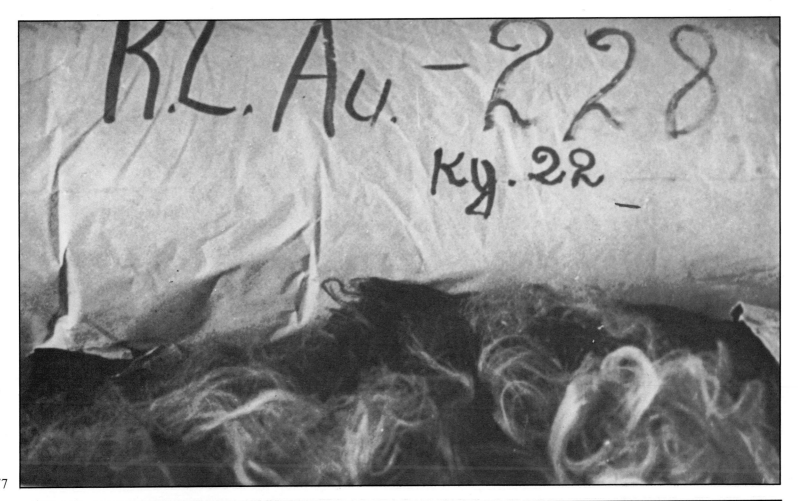

77

78

17

18

179
Auschwitz II-Birkenau. View of Jewish prisoners whom the SS considered fit for forced labour, in one of the compounds of BII that was not exclusively for Jews. In many parts of Auschwitz, the Jews lived and worked alongside other prisoners: they died alongside them too. (Photo taken by the SS, 1944)

180
Auschwitz II-Birkenau. The deserted railway ramp after the Jews have been led away. Only their property remains behind. (Photo taken by the SS, 1944)

181
Auschwitz. Property brought to Auschwitz by deportees was plundered by the SS. It was first taken to special warehouses —'Canada', in camp jargon. There were two areas known as 'Canada': 'Canada I', near Auschwitz I, and 'Canada II', a much larger section, in Auschwitz II-Birkenau. (Photo taken by the SS, 1944)

182
Property plundered from deportees waiting to be stored in the warehouses of 'Canada I', near Auschwitz I. (Photo taken by the SS, 1944)

183
Jewish women and children on the way to their death in the gas chambers of Auschwitz II-Birkenau. (Photo taken by the SS, 1944)

181

182

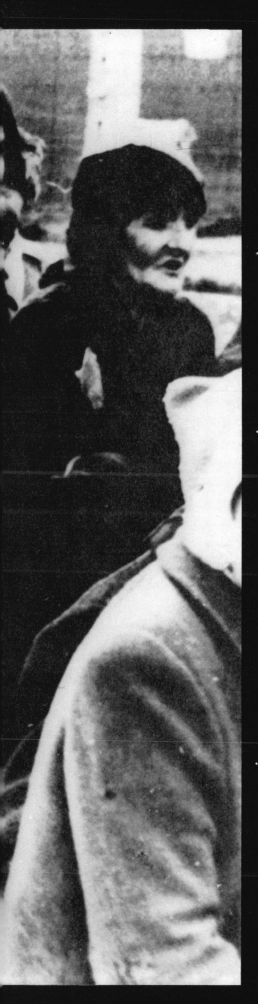

When the transports of Jews were unloaded, all their baggage was left on the ramp until all the Jews had been taken to the extermination places or into the camp. Afterwards, a special transport squad took all the baggage to 'Canada', the place where it was sorted . . .

Even though additional sheds and barracks were constantly being built and prisoners were sorting day and night in ever-increasing numbers, and even though many freight wagons—often as many as twenty a day—were loaded with items that had been sorted, piles of unsorted baggage still remained. . . .

Hardly had thirty new barracks been built when they were filled to capacity, with big heaps of unsorted baggage piled between them.

When the sorting after a major operation had been finished, valuables and money were packed into trunks and sent to Berlin by lorry, first to the WVHA [the Economic Administration Head Office of the SS], and from there to the Reichsbank. The Reichsbank had a special section dealing exclusively with items from the Jewish actions.[1] Eichmann told me one day that the valuables and foreign currencies were traded in Switzerland, and that indeed the entire Swiss market for valuables was flooded with them. More ordinary watches were sent in their thousands to Sachsenhausen. . . .

Gold teeth were melted into ingots by the dentists in the SS quarters and sent monthly to the SS Sanitary Head Office. Precious stones of immeasurable value were also found in tooth fillings and extracted. Women's hair was supplied to a factory in Bavaria to be used in the armaments industry.

Rudolf Höss

---

[1] The usual Nazi term for anti-Jewish actions.

184
Auschwitz II-Birkenau. Property plundered from deportees was sent to the heart of the Reich, where it was distributed among institutions and civilians. This particular shipment, awaiting dispatch, was found on the liberation of the camp.
(H. Makarewicz, 1945)

185–6
Auschwitz II-Birkenau. Sorting plundered property outside buildings in 'Canada II'. (Photos taken by the SS, 1944)

187
Auschwitz II-Birkenau. Bundles of *taleisim* (ritual shawls worn by Jewish men) found after the camp's liberation. (Photo taken during an inspection after the camp's liberation, 1945)

184

185

186

The following three photographs (188–90) were taken clandestinely inside Auschwitz II-Birkenau by prisoners. They are the only photographs taken by prisoners that have survived. For such clandestine photography to have been possible, film had to be smuggled into the camp, the photographs had to be taken—with extreme caution, because of the danger involved—and the film then had to be smuggled back out of the camp. The operation was the product of collaboration between Polish political prisoners and prisoners from the Sonderkommando, a special unit of Jewish prisoners whose job it was to burn the bodies of people who had been gassed. A note smuggled out of the camp with the photographs on 4 September 1944 by two Polish political prisoners, Józef Cyrankiewicz and Stanisław Kłodziński, described what they showed and requested more film.

'Urgent. Send two iron reels of film ($2^1/_2$ x $3^1/_2$ in.) as soon as possible. It is possible to take pictures. We send you photographs from Birkenau—people who have been gassed. The photograph shows a heap of bodies piled outdoors. Bodies were burned outdoors when the crematorium could not keep pace with the number of bodies to be burned. In the foreground are bodies ready to be thrown on the heap. Another photograph shows one of the places in the forest where people were told to undress, allegedly for a bath, but in fact before being driven to the gas chambers. Send a reel as soon as possible. Send the enclosed photographs to Tell.'[1]

[1] The note is now in the archives of the Auschwitz State Museum (Materials on the Camp's Resistance Movement, ii. 136). 'Tell' was Teresa Lasocka-Estreicher, a member of the Cracow underground aid committee for prisoners of concentration camps.

188
Jewish women being driven naked to Gas Chamber V. Victims were sometimes made to undress in the open air and go naked into the building where they were to be murdered. (Photo taken clandestinely, probably by Alex, a Greek Jew, in 1944)

189–90
Auschwitz II-Birkenau. Bodies of people who had been gassed being burned in the open air by Jewish prisoners from the Sonderkommando. (Photos taken clandestinely, probably by Alex, a Greek Jew, in 1944)

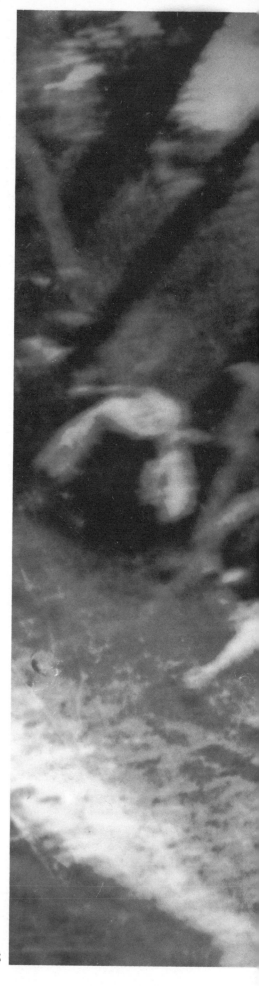

188

Prisoners trying to retain their human dignity behind the barbed wire of the camp waged an unequal struggle against the SS. In a note smuggled out of the camp, Józef Cyrankiewicz, a Polish political prisoner, wrote: 'Though living in the camps of slavery—[we are] free in spirit. We send to the free world information about our existence, about our unequal struggle for the rights of political prisoners. We are behind the wires, but as soldiers and as members of our nations we demand human rights.'

One of the essential objectives of the resistance in the camp was keeping records of what was happening and reporting SS atrocities. Thanks to contacts established with Poles beyond the barbed wire, information about the camp was conveyed to the outside world. Stanisław Kłodziński, a Polish political prisoner, wrote in a note of 20 June 1943 which was smuggled out of the camp: 'Our messages should be transmitted abroad in great quantities, as the Germans would then become convinced that the world is informed about Auschwitz.'

A note dated 16 September 1944 headed 'Auschwitz Executioners' gave the names and identifying features of the SS personnel of Auschwitz, starting with Rudolf Höss, the camp's commandant. 'We send rough descriptions of Auschwitz executioners. All the data are authentic beyond doubt. London should pronounce death sentences on these murderers as soon as possible.'

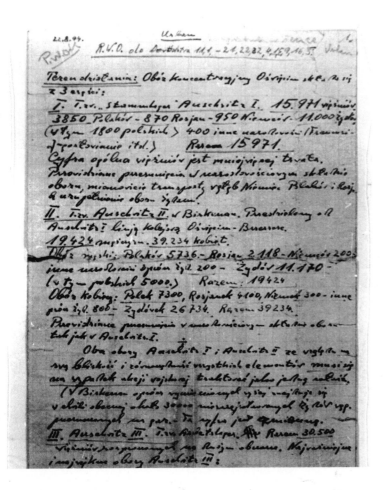

191
Copies of clandestine reports prepared mostly by Polish prisoners and smuggled out of the camp. Reports of this kind provided the outside world with information about the number of deportees, nationalities of prisoners, conditions in the camp, and the mass murder of the Jews, and identified the most brutal SS men.

Rezolucja więźniów politycznych

Jako więźniowie polityczni hitlerowskich obozów koncentracyjnych piętnujemy wobec całego świata kłamliwe i cyniczne odezwanie się przewodniczącego t. zw. "Volksgerichtu" hitlerowskiego sądzącego niemieckich generałów w związku z wydarzeniami 20 lipca.

W odpowiedzi na ujawniony zamiar niemieckiego feldmarszałka Witzlebena, zaaresztowania załóg pilniejszych obozów koncentracyjnych i zwolnienia znajdujących się tam więźniów, wyraził się przewodniczący tego "sądu" ... [nieczytelne] dla skompromitowania planów ... wielkiego Witzlebena wobec ... narodu niemieckiego, że chodziło tu o "zwolnienie czysto kryminalnych ...

Ponieważ takie cyniczne określenie więźniów politycznych jako "czysto kryminalnych ..." może też służyć do usprawiedliwienia wobec własnego narodu wszelkich ...

Frauenlager

26.3.42	-49 - 099	Üb. Rav...
	1000 - 1998	
28.3.42	1999 - 2796	
2.4.42	2797 - 3761	
5.4.42	3762	Münch
8.4.42	3763 - 4760	
13.4.42	4761 - 5203	
17.4.42	5204 - 5230	
-"-	5231 - 5232	Oppeln
19.4.42	5233 - 5768	
23.4.42	5769 - 6225	
24.4.42	6226 - 6783	
27.4.42	6784 - 6910	Krak
29.4.42	6911 - 7407	
1.5.42	7408 - 7431	Krak
	7432 - 7433	Trop...
6.5.42	7434 - 7447	K...
12.5.42	7448 - 7453	Üb. Rav...
15.5.42	7454	Chm...
18.5.42	7455	Kat...
20.5.42	7456	Oppeln
-"-	7457 - 7469	Prag
22.5.42	7470 - 7478	Sand
28.5.42	7479 - 7532	Krak
30.5.42	7533 - 7534	Bres...
-"-	7535 - 7585	Krak k
5.6.42	7586 - 7596	Katt
-"-	7597 - 7601	Sam
6.6.42	7602 - 7606	Sam
10.6.42	7607 - 7608	Sam
12.6.42	7609 - 7618	Sam
13.6.42	7619 - 7620	Katt
17.6.42	7621 - 7626	Katt
-"-	7627 - 7671	Prag
19.6.42	7672 - 7677	Sam
20.6.42	7678 - 7932	
-"-	7933 - 7957	Üb. Rav...
22.6.42	7958	Oppeln
24.6.42	7959 - 7960	Samm...
-"-	7961 - 8026	

(76)

1940.			
20.5./	1 - 30	Sachs.	
11.6./	31 - 758	Kra-Tam.	
16.6/	759 - 1071		
22.6/	1072 - 1094	Ratt.	
24.6/	1095 - 1131	-"-	
25.6/	1132 - 1221	-"-	
26.6/	1222 - 1263	-"-	
27.6/	1264 - 1282	-"-	
6.7/	1283 - 1342	-"-	
11.7/	1343 - 1354	-"-	
14.7/	1355 - 1419	Kra.	
24.7/	1420	Katt.	
	1421 - 1438		
6.8/	1439 - 1441		
8.8/	1442 - 1484		
	1485		
	1486 - 1542		
	1543 - 1899	Vas.	
15.8./	1900	Katt.	
18.7/	1901 - 3479	Vas.	
	3480	Katt.	
27.8/	3481 - 3485	Katt	
	3486 - 3487		
	3488 - 3587	Sachs.	
30.8/	3588	Katt.	
30.8/	3589 - 3698	Kra-Tarnow	
30.8/	3699 - 3700		
30.8/	3701 - 3707	Kra-Tarnow	
2.9.	3708 - 3729	Katt.	
30.8/	3730	Kra-Tarnow	
5.9./	3731 - 3738	Katt.	
6.9./	3739 - 3757	Katt	
7.9./	3758 - 3772		
10.9./	3773		
11.9/	3774	Oss.	
4.9/	3775	Katt.	

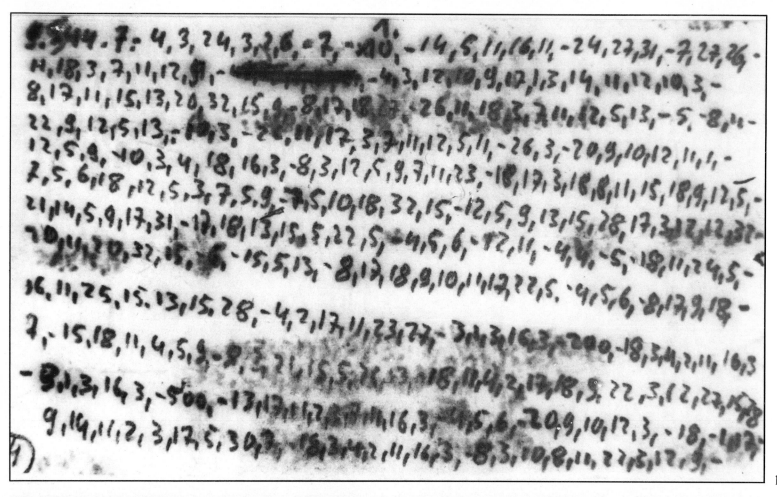

19

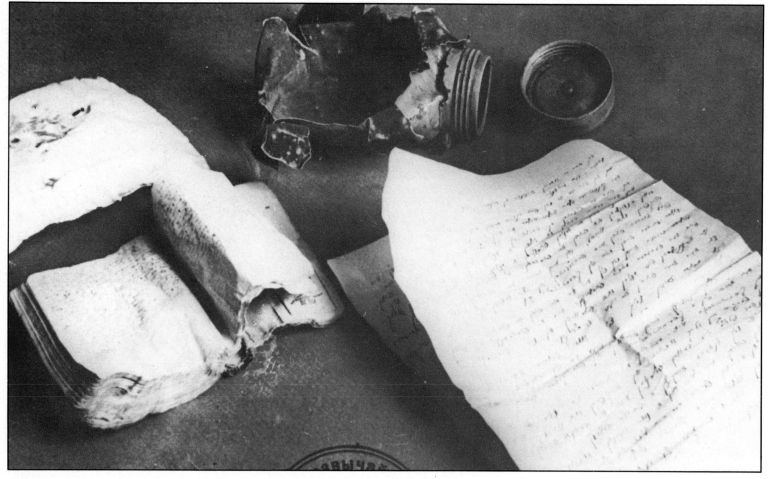

19.

[180]

192

Coded message written by Stanisław Kłodziński, a member of the camp resistance movement, on 9 October 1944, and smuggled out of the camp. It described the revolt of Jewish prisoners from the Sonder-kommando. '9 October 1944. The Sonderkommando, those who burn the bodies of people who had been gassed, were themselves to have been gassed on Saturday, the 7th of this month. However, they were not gassed because, facing their inevitable death, they attacked the SS . . . One of the crematoria was set on fire.'

This revolt, which succeeded in putting Gas Chamber and Cremat-orium IV completely out of action, was the only planned revolt using weapons or explosives that ever took place in Auschwitz. The 450 Sonderkommando who took part in it were shot by the SS: 250 during the revolt itself and 200 subsequently. The Polish Jew who had master-minded the operation, Jankiel (Yankel) Handelsman, and the four Jewish women, led by Rosa Robota, who had smuggled in the explosives, were subsequently tortured by the SS: the women were later hanged, and Handelsman died under interrogation. The hanging of the four women on 6 January 1945 was the last public execution to take place before the camp was liberated.

193

After the war, a description of the process of mass murder carried out in Auschwitz II-Birkenau was found in 1945 in an aluminium flask that had been buried in the vicinity of Gas Chamber and Crematorium II. It had been written in Yiddish by Zalmen Gradowski, a Jewish prisoner from the Sonderkommando. The photo shows this flask and a portion of the text.

194

Flask containing a manuscript written by another Jewish prisoner from the Sonderkommando, Zalmen Lewental. It was discovered seventeen years after the war was over in the area of Gas Chamber and Crematorium III in Auschwitz II-Birkenau. (Z. Łoboda, 1962)

194

195

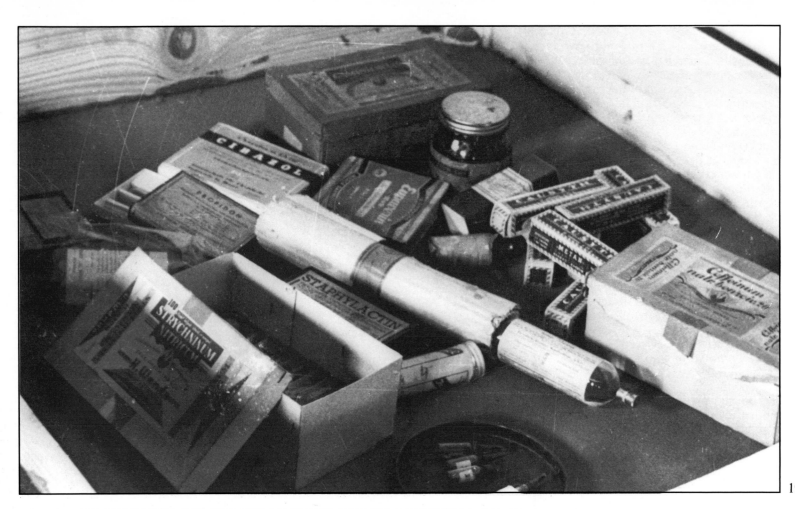

31.VIII.42

Otrzymałem około
1000 ampułek rozmaitych
lekarstw. (Coramina, Oligipu-
natum, Calc. glic. i. t. d.)
Wszystko dostarczone na izbę
chorych w K.L.Au.

J Śmietański
253

[182]

195

Manuscript by Zalmen Lewental containing information about the revolt by Jews from the Sonderkommando and about other manuscripts hidden in Auschwitz II-Birkenau. (Z. Łoboda, 1962)

196

Medical supplies were smuggled into the camp, mainly by Poles living close by. (Photographer unknown)

197–8

Messages sent by Janusz Skrzetuski (Pogonowski) and Edward Biernacki, Polish political prisoners, confirming the receipt of medical supplies from Poles living near the camp.

199

Radio made clandestinely by prisoners working in the *Fahrbereitschaft* (machine workshop).

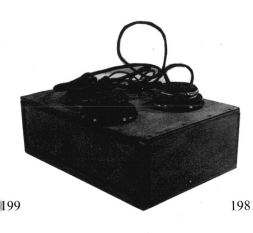

199

198

200

201

202

200
Nazi record books of the Gypsy camp in Auschwitz II-Birkenau, discovered after the camp was liberated. They had been buried by Tadeusz Joachimowski, a Polish political prisoner, in an effort to preserve evidence of Nazi crimes. Some 21,000 Gypsies are listed there by name.

201
Prisoners often tried to escape. Most attempts ended tragically. The photo shows a dead prisoner in front of an electrified perimeter fence in Auschwitz. We shall never know whether he was shot trying to escape or had decided to commit suicide by throwing himself at the fence. Even the fact that he appears to have been wearing regular civilian clothes proves nothing: when prison uniforms were in short supply, the clothes of murdered deportees would be used instead with a coloured stripe or stripes painted down the back for ease of identification. (Photo taken by the SS, date unknown)

202
Although most attempted escapes ended tragically, those organized with the help of the local Polish underground were often successful. The photo shows a group of men who succeeded in escaping—from the left: Mieczysław Januszewski, Otto Küssel, Bolesław Kuczbara, and the artist Jan Baraś-Komski (standing; his pictures appear later in this volume). The man second on the right is Andrzej Harat, a member of the Polish resistance; the woman is a relative of his from Libiąż, near Oświęcim, who had helped hide the group. (J. Korpal, 1942)

203
'Teodor' partisans of the combat organization of the Polish Socialist Party. The partisans included former prisoners who had escaped from Auschwitz: from the left, Kazimierz Szwemberg, Tadeusz Uszyński, and Jerzy Tabeau. (Photographer unknown, 1944; photo taken outside a hostel on Babia Góra, near Zawoja)

03

EXECUTIVE OFFICE OF THE PRESIDENT

★WAR REFUGEE BOARD

WASHINGTON . D. C.

4

204

Some of the prisoners who escaped from Auschwitz wrote testimonies about what was happening there, a few of which were published in the West before the war was over. This is a page from a report about Auschwitz issued in Washington D.C. in November 1944 that presented eye-witness accounts by some Jewish prisoners who had managed to escape—Rudolph Vrba, Alfred Wetzler, Czesław Mordowicz, and Arnost Rosin—and Jerzy Tabeau, a Polish political prisoner (referred to in the text opposite as a 'Polish major').

GERMAN EXTERMINATION CAMPS — AUSCHWITZ AND BIRKENAU

It is a fact beyond denial that the Germans have deliberately and systematically murdered millions of innocent civilians — Jews and Christians alike — all over Europe. This campaign of terror and brutality, which is unprecedented in all history and which even now continues unabated, is part of the German plan to subjugate the free peoples of the world.

So revolting and diabolical are the German atrocities that the minds of civilized people find it difficult to believe that they have actually taken place. But the governments of the United States and of other countries have evidence which clearly substantiates the facts.

The War Refugee Board is engaged in a desperate effort to save as many as possible of Hitler's intended victims. To facilitate its work the Board has representatives in key spots in Europe. These representatives have tested contacts throughout Europe and keep the Board fully advised concerning the German campaign of extermination and torture.

Recently the Board received from a representative close to the scene two eye-witness accounts of events which occurred in notorious extermination camps established by the Germans. The first report is based upon the experiences of two young Slovakian Jews who escaped in April, 1944 after spending two years in the Nazi concentration camps at Auschwitz and Birkenau in southwestern Poland. The second report is made by a non-Jewish Polish major, 204 the only survivor of one group imprisoned at Auschwitz.

[185]

205

206

Resistance in Auschwitz also found its expression in the clandestine composition of poems, songs, and prayers; drawings of daily life in the camp and of fellow-prisoners were made on scraps of paper and card.

205
Arrival of a Transport of Jews at Auschwitz. The picture is taken from a notebook containing twenty-two drawings that was found in the infirmary compound of Auschwitz II-Birkenau (BII*f*) in 1947. It had been concealed in a bottle placed under the wooden floor of a barrack and covered with a piece of wood. (Pencil on paper, 6 x 8 in., artist and year unknown)

206
Returning from Work. The prisoners are carrying one of their number who had died or been killed while working. (Pencil on cardboard, 10 x 13 in., Mieczysław Kościelniak, 1942)

207
Portrait of Mala Zimetbaum, a Jewish woman from Belgium (prisoner number 19880). In 1944, she and a Polish political prisoner, Edward Galiński (prisoner number 531), escaped from the camp. They were caught after two weeks and sentenced to death. (Coloured pencil on cardboard, 10 x 7 in., Zofia Stępień-Bator, 1944)

208
Portrait of Jan Brabec, a Czech political prisoner (prisoner number 25565). He died in the camp on 27 March 1942, a victim of typhus. (Pencil on paper, 11 x 12 in., Stanisław Gutkiewicz, 1942)

209
Portrait of Kazimierz Jarzębowski, a Polish political prisoner (prisoner number 115) who belonged to the camp resistance movement. In 1943, he tried to escape but was captured and then shot at the wall of executions in Auschwitz I (Pencil on paper, 9 x 6 in., Jan Baraś-Komski, 1940; the artist himself succeeded in escaping: see Caption 202)

210
Portrait of Géza Schein, a Hungarian Jew (prisoner number 103820). Géza Schein gave this portrait to Emilia Klimczyk, a Polish woman who sometimes helped a group of Jewish prisoners working in the Brzeszcze mine by bringing them some extra food. (Pencil on paper, 6 x 4 in., Jan Markiel, 1944)

[186]

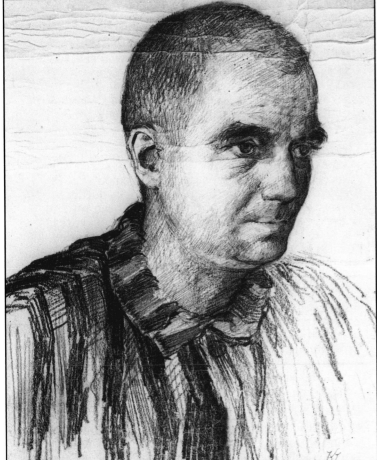

07
08

09
10

[187]

211

211

Portrait of Helena Plotnicka. The portrait of this Polish woman was made in Auschwitz and given to her as a token of gratitude for her help to prisoners. In 1943, she was arrested for her activities and sent to the camp. She died there on 17 March 1944. (Wooden bas-relief, 11 x 8 in.; artist unknown, 1940–2)

212

Portrait of Witold Pilecki, known in the camp as Tomasz Serafiński (prisoner number 4859), who was a member of the Polish resistance movement. On 15 September 1940, he let himself be caught during a round-up in Warsaw so that he could get into Auschwitz and establish an underground network there. Once in Auschwitz, he became one of the leaders of the resistance movement. In April 1943, he escaped from the camp to continue his activity in the Polish underground and wrote a number of reports about conditions in Auschwitz. He later joined the Polish army, fighting on the western front in Italy under General Anders. At the end of 1945 he returned to Poland but was then arrested by the Communist authorities as an enemy of the state. He was tried and sentenced to death, and executed in 1948. (Pencil on paper, 11 x 8 in, Stanisław Gutkiewicz, 1942)

213

A Christmas tree made clandestinely in the women's camp. (Military cloth, ribbon, wood, and paper, height 16 in., Leokadia Szymańska, 1944)

213

In the face of forthcoming defeat, the Nazis began to hide the traces of their crimes. A report by the Cracow underground aid committee for prisoners of concentration camps stated: 'The camp's Gestapo [Politische Abteilung] is destroying documents—evidence of its terrible unpunished crimes—by burning them in a former crematorium. The whole operation aimed at removing traces continues.' Pery Broad described the last days of Auschwitz as follows: 'In the middle of January 1945, Auschwitz was evacuated in wild panic. All prisoners able to walk were taken off to concentration camps deep inside Germany, where the majority were liberated about three months later. Sick prisoners were left behind to their fate in Auschwitz and in its sub-camps. They were to have been shot but at the last moment the SS officers were scared and did not give the order. Personal documents were set on fire outside all the administration buildings in Auschwitz. As for the buildings in which the greatest mass murders in the history of mankind were committed, they were blown up.'

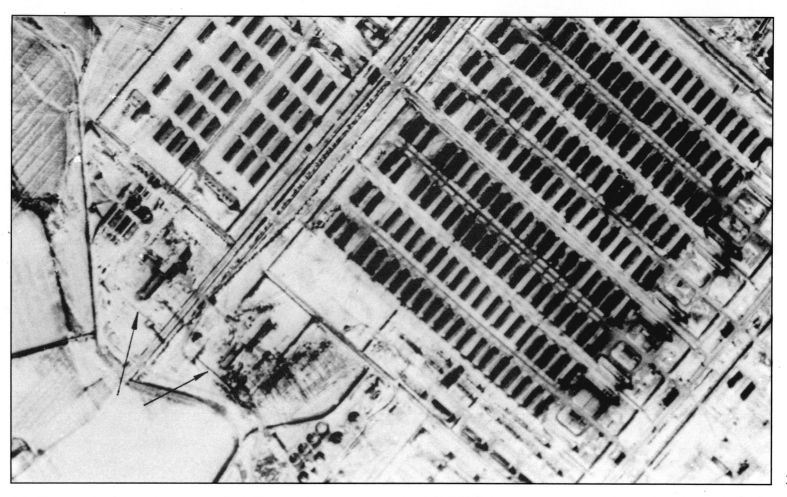

2

2

[190]

214
Auschwitz II-Birkenau. Gas
Chambers and Crematoria II and III
(arrowed) were partially dismantled
before the camp was evacuated. The
roof over the undressing rooms of
both buildings (just beyond the tip of
each arrow) had already been
removed. (Aerial photo taken by the
Allies on 21 Dec. 1944)

215–17
Auschwitz II-Birkenau. Not having
time to dismantle the gas chambers
and crematoria completely, the SS
blew them up before leaving the
camp. (Photos 215 and 216:
S. Mucha, 1945; photo 217:
H. Makarewicz, 1945)

216

217

218

Auschwitz II-Birkenau. Part of a destroyed incinerator in Gas Chamber and Crematorium V; the small door through which the ashes were removed (see photo 169) is clearly visible. (H. Makarewicz, 1945)

219

Auschwitz II-Birkenau. Ruins of Gas Chamber and Crematorium V. (H. Makarewicz, 1945)

218

219

220

Auschwitz II-Birkenau. Warehouses that had been used to store plundered property before sending it to the interior of the Reich were set on fire by the SS before they left the camp. (H. Makarewicz, 1945)

221

Auschwitz I. After the camp's liberation: the scene inside a room containing camp records. (S. Łuczko, 1945)

222

Auschwitz II-Birkenau. The Nazis evacuated about 60,000 prisoners into the Reich a few days before the camp's liberation, conscious that they were living witnesses to the atrocities that they had committed. Only the sick, the weak, and the corpses (shown here) were left behind. (H. Makarewicz, 1945)

220

221

222

223

Body of a woman murdered by the SS during the evacuation of Auschwitz. The last groups of prisoners evacuated from Auschwitz had to march for several days in the depths of winter before reaching their final destination—the railway station in Wodzisław Śląski, 60 kilometres away. Here prisoners who had been evacuated from all sections of the Auschwitz complex were regrouped and then transported away from the front line by train. Hundreds of prisoners died during the march from hunger, beatings, and extreme cold. Those who were no longer able to march, or who tried to escape, were shot by their SS guards. (Photographer unknown, 1945)

224

Ćwiklice. One of the mass graves containing the bodies of evacuated prisoners who had died or been killed by the SS during the march from Auschwitz. The route of the death march had many such graves. After the war, monuments were erected at these sites by local people, who continue to look after them to this day. (Photographer unknown, 1945)

223

224

225

Some of the prisoners evacuated from Auschwitz were transported over long distances in open freight cars and died en route of exposure and starvation. This transport was photographed as it left Kolina railway station in occupied Czechoslovakia on 24 January 1945. (Jindřich Kremer, 1945)

225

226

Bielszowice. These eight men, former prisoners of Auschwitz III-Monowitz, managed to escape during the evacuation. (Photographer unknown, 1945)

227

At the main gate of Auschwitz I: The liberation of Auschwitz by Soviet soldiers of the 60th Army of the First Ukrainian Front. (Photo taken from the Soviet film *Chronicle of the Liberation of Auschwitz*, 1945)

226

227

228-35
Not all prisoners left behind alive by the Nazis lived to see the liberation. (Photos 228-9, 231: S. Mucha, 1945; photos 230, 234-5: taken from the Soviet film *Chronicle of the Liberation of Auschwitz*, 1945; photos 232-3: H. Makarewicz, 1945)

228

229

230

231

[197]

236–7
Oświęcim. The solemn funeral, on 28 February 1945, of people found dead in Auschwitz when it was liberated and those who died there after the liberation. (Photos taken from the Soviet film *Chronicle of the Liberation of Auschwitz*, 1945)

234

23

6

7

[201]

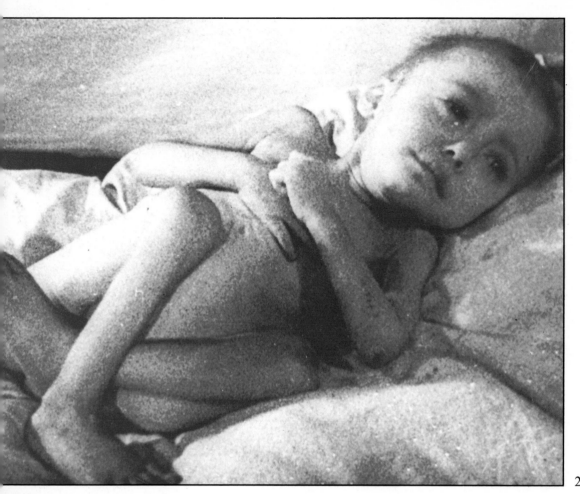

238–45
Auschwitz II-Birkenau. About 7,000 prisoners, including more than 600 children and young people below the age of 18, were alive when the camp was liberated. A further 500 prisoners were found alive in various Auschwitz sub-camps. (Photos taken from the Soviet film *Chronicle of the Liberation of Auschwitz*, 1945)

238

239

40

41

24

24

244

245

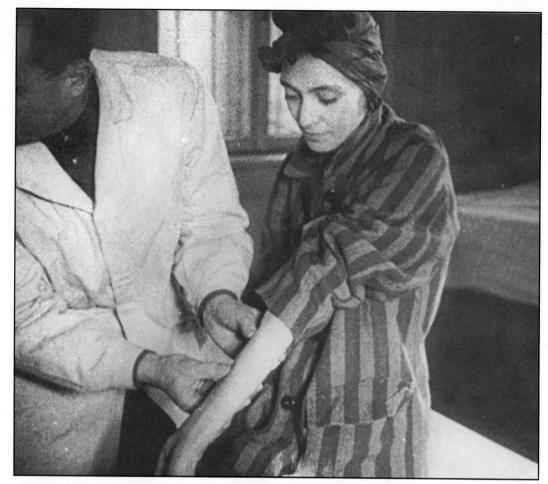

246
Nazi doctors had experimented on this woman by injecting poisonous substances into her veins. (Photo taken from the Soviet film *Chronicle of the Liberation of Auschwitz*, 1945)

247
Auschwitz survivor being examined by a Soviet medical board. (Photo taken from the Soviet film *Chronicle of the Liberation of Auschwitz*, 1945)

246

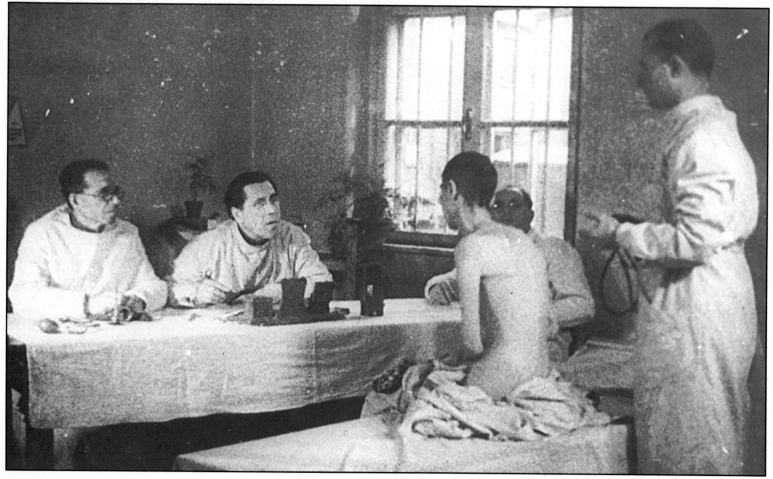

247

248

Evidence of Nazi medical
experiments connected with skin
grafting. (Photo taken from the
Soviet film *Chronicle of the
Liberation of Auschwitz*, 1945)

249

Women's ward of the hospital set up
by the Polish Red Cross after the
camp's liberation. (Photographer
unknown, 1945)

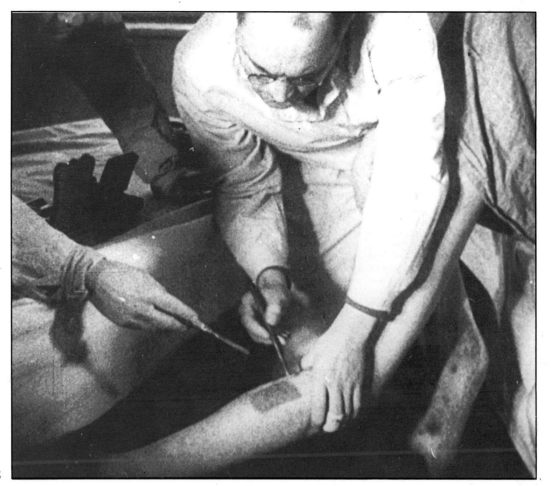

248

249

250–1
Auschwitz II-Birkenau. Mass grave photographed by the Soviet army after the camp's liberation. (Photos taken from the Soviet film *Chronicle of the Liberation of Auschwitz*, 1945)

250

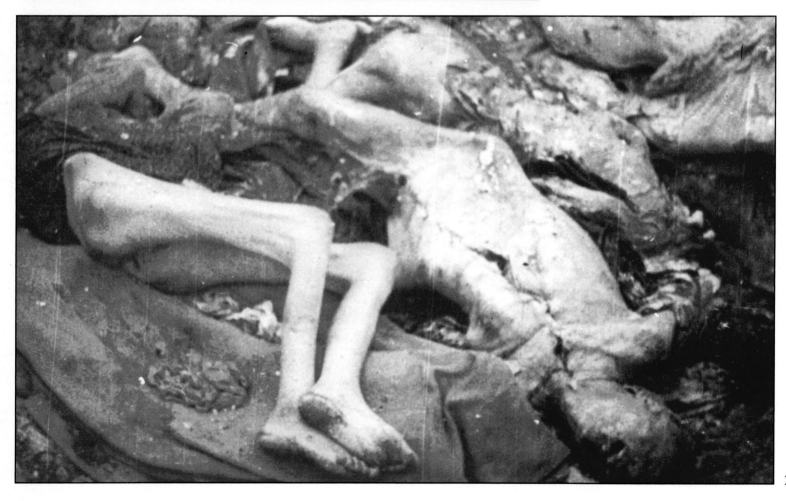

251

252–3
A British delegation headed by Dr Hewlett Johnson, Dean of Canterbury Cathedral (with clerical collar, fourth on right), during an inspection of a warehouse containing the spectacles of people who had been murdered. (Photo 252: S. Kolowca, 1945; photo 253: taken from the Soviet film *Chronicle of the Liberation of Auschwitz*, 1945)

252

253

254

253

254

Auschwitz II-Birkenau. Dr Hewlett Johnson (centre) and other members of a British delegation being taken round prisoners' barracks by Professor Jan Sehn, a Polish examining magistrate (first on the left). (S. Kolowca, 1945)

255

Artificial limbs taken from invalids murdered in Auschwitz. (S. Mucha, 1945)

256-7

Inspection of a warehouse in Auschwitz containing the hair of women and girls. (Photo 256: taken from the Soviet film *Chronicle of the Liberation of Auschwitz*, 1945; photo 257: S. Kolowca, 1945)

256

257

תרצ"ה-1935

20763/25

A32·363

PAMIĄTKA 1ej KOMUNJI ŚW.

258
Family photographs brought to Auschwitz in the personal possessions of people destined to be murdered.

259–65
Auschwitz II-Birkenau. Property brought by people deported to Auschwitz. (Photo 259: Z. Łoboda; photos 260–1: taken from the Soviet film *Chronicle of the Liberation of Auschwitz*, 1945; photos 262–5: taken during an inspection after the camp's liberation, 1945)

259

60

261

26

263

264

265

Above. Prisoner number 26352: Irina
Midlet, a Russian political prisoner
who was brought to Auschwitz on
2 December 1942. Fate unknown.

Opposite. Prisoner number 33164:
Ludwik Puget, a Polish political
prisoner, an artist, painter, and
sculptor who was born in Cracow in
1877. He was arrested in Cracow
during a round-up while sitting in
a café frequented by artists, and then
deported to Auschwitz on 25 April
1942. He was shot at the Wall of
Executions on 27 May 1942.

The Art Inspired
by Auschwitz

LIFE and death in the Auschwitz murder camp inspired works of art in a variety of forms. Events and scenes from the daily reality of Auschwitz found powerful expression in the plastic arts, literature, poetry, films, and music. The Auschwitz theme continues to inspire a very wide artistic circle, but here we shall consider only examples of the important body of material produced by people who experienced Auschwitz personally.

The works presented here have been selected from those held by the Auschwitz–Birkenau State Museum because they reconstruct and represent everyday occurrences in Auschwitz that are not adequately covered in the photographs that make up the main part of this volume. If it were possible to use them to create a chronicle of all the days and nights in the camp, of all the cruelty, inhumanity, and suffering in Auschwitz, it would be only the dates and the faces that would change; the events themselves would be endlessly repeated.

Each of the pictures and drawings reproduced in the following pages was created by a former Auschwitz prisoner. Some were actually made in the camp. It hardly seems possible that human values and artistic energies could have been maintained in the wretched conditions of an environment whose main goal was systematic murder—conditions deliberately designed to dehumanize prisoners and deprive them of the reflexes, customs, and habits of civilized life—but hundreds of testimonies, including memoirs written by former prisoners, show that this was not the case. Even in the most terrible of situations, artists found ways to rise above their experiences and communicate the stirrings of the soul. In doing so, they left evidence of their existence for succeeding generations. Even when only pencils and scraps of paper or cardboard were all that was available, they were able to draw scenes from camp life and create caricatures or portraits of their fellow-prisoners.

In fact, very few of the works made in the camp portrayed scenes from camp life, because this was forbidden; most therefore are representations of former realities beyond the barbed wire that now were only dreams. Looking at these paintings, one wonders how people living amidst bestiality and brutality were able to give such lyrical expression to their yearning for an existence that must have seemed so remote, so totally unattainable. One example of this is the work of Bronisław Czech, an Olympic sportsman who came from the mountains of Zakopane in southern Poland and managed to re-create them even in Auschwitz.

The works that were created in the camp can be broadly divided into three types: those created at the order of the SS; those created with the knowledge of the SS; and those created clandestinely. Unfortunately, much of the work created did not survive; much of what did was of the first type, created as a consequence of

Bronisław Czech, *Morskie Oko*. Oil on canvas, 20 x 28 in., 1942.

a remarkable decision taken early in 1941 to establish a camp museum in Auschwitz.

The circumstances that led to the establishment of the museum were a matter of chance—like so much else in Auschwitz. During an inspection of the carpentry workshops, the camp's commandant, Rudolf Höss, noticed a prisoner drawing a picture of a horse. Höss, a horse-lover, started to talk to him. Seeing a chance to better his situation, the prisoner—a Pole called Franciszek Targosz—suggested the idea of establishing a collection that would include objects found in the homes of Poles deported from Oświęcim, as well as articles brought to Auschwitz by prisoners in their luggage. Höss liked the idea and ordered Targosz to set about organizing it.

Targosz was given the use of premises, provided with display boards, stands, and showcases, and allowed to employ prisoners to work with him. The showcases were soon filled with an

[220]

interesting assortment: coins, pottery, metal objects, military accessories, items of clothing, and ritual objects of various religions and denominations.

Targosz also managed to obtain permission to employ a few artist-prisoners to work in the museum in a more creative capacity. Paintings were in effect commissioned—on the theme of freedom, for example—and given by Höss to various dignitaries visiting Auschwitz or kept for his own pleasure. Taking advantage of Höss's keen interest, Targosz gradually managed to make the museum a kind of asylum that was able to afford some artist-prisoners a measure of protection and shelter and allow them time for their artistic expression. Scores of paintings, sculptures, and craft objects were made in this way. Several have survived to this day and are now housed in the collections of the Auschwitz–Birkenau State Museum.

The prisoners' artistic output played a role in their struggle for survival because it brought them recognition from other prisoners as well as protection from SS men who wanted them to produce works of art for themselves and their friends. Confirmation that this practice existed is found in an order (Order 24/43 of the garrison commander, dated 8 July 1943) in which Höss forbids the practice of ordering prisoners to make 'pictures or other so-called pieces of art, for example, tin roses, etc.', on the grounds that it was wasteful: 'Prisoners not only do work of no use, but materials obtained with great difficulty are being wasted.' He warned that he would ask the SS Reichsführer to punish any SS officer who might dare to 'order or permit' such futile work, 'regardless of who he is and what his rank is'. However, this order was evidently never implemented, even by the garrison commander himself, because it was quite clear that both the camp's commandant and other SS officers ordered the prisoners to make such objects and had them in their apartments.

Objects of artistic merit also came to be produced in the camp's workshops, where prisoners employed as carpenters, glaziers, and metalworkers had access to materials. Here, too, works were made for SS officers, though sometimes apparently also to satisfy the prisoners' own inner needs. An example of the latter found in the camp after the liberation is a miniature coffin (6 x $1^1/_2$ x $1^1/_2$ in.) in black wood, with an emaciated male figure in light wood on the top; a series of pinpricks at the foot of the coffin read '27-1-1917—16-1-1942'. Inside is a small fragment of charred bone. This tragic ensemble may well have been made to mark the

Sarcophagus (artist unknown). Wood, 6 x $1^1/_2$ x $1^1/_2$ in., 1942 (?). View of pin-pricked dates.

death of a prisoner's friend or relative; we have no way of knowing.

Most of the works reproduced in this volume, however, were made in quite different circumstances. After the liberation, many former prisoners who were artists sought to re-create the scenes that Auschwitz had engraved in their hearts and minds—some-

Sarcophagus (artist unknown). Wood, 6 x $1^1/_2$ x $1^1/_2$ in., 1942 (?). View of carved figure on lid.

thing they had been forbidden to do in Auschwitz itself. It was as if by externalizing what they had witnessed—the appalling events, the gas chambers, the crematorium incinerators—they would perpetuate the memory of those who had suffered and died, while at the same time ridding themselves of the dark memories that tormented their souls.

In selecting the paintings and drawings for this volume, emphasis has been placed on portraying the brutality of everyday life in the concentration camp. Unlike the scenes shown in the photographs earlier in this volume, these pictures depict the sadism of the Nazi guards and those prisoners (*kapos*) who assisted them in their duties. The result is a terrifying witness to the horrors that ordinary prisoners had to endure, and proof that documents are not the only form of indictment against the Nazis. The works presented here spell out an accusation no less powerful. Each brush stroke and pencil mark is a condemnation of the Nazi system, a visual reminder that never again must humanity be allowed to sink to such depravity.

Kazimierz Smoleń

[222]

Władysław Siwek, *A Group of New Arrivals*. Pen and ink, 28 x 40 in., 1950.

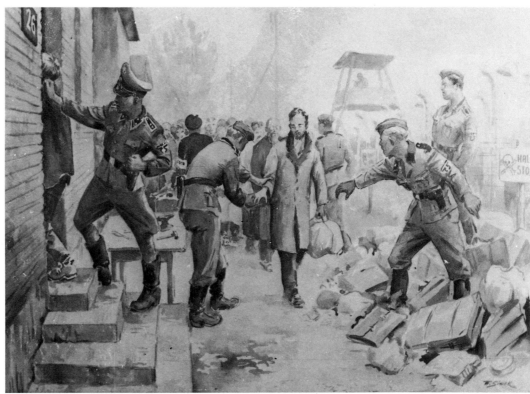

Top: Władysław Siwek, *Robbing New Arrivals of their Property.* Water-colour, 28 x 40 in., 1950.

Bottom: Mieczysław Kościelniak, *Tattooing Prisoners.* Pen and ink, 28 x 40 in., 1972.

Top: Mieczysław Kościelniak, *Inside a Barrack in Auschwitz II-Birkenau.* Pen and ink, 28 x 40 in., 1972.

Bottom: Mieczysław Kościelniak, *Night* (from the 'Day of a Prisoner' cycle). Pen and ink, 32 x 26 in., 1950.

Jerzy Potrzebowski, *Getting Up in the Morning*. Water-colour, 28 x 40 in., 1950.

Top: Jerzy Potrzebowski, *Washing under a Pump in 1940*. Water-colour, 24 x 26 in., 1950.

Bottom: Jerzy Potrzebowski, *Washing in a Bathhouse in 1941*. Water-colour, 24 x 26 in., 1950.

Mieczysław Kościelniak, *Getting Up in the Morning* (from the 'Day of a Woman Prisoner' cycle). Pen and ink, 26 x 32 in., 1950.

[229]

Jan Baraś-Komski was born in Bircza on 3 February 1915 and studied at the Cracow Academy of Fine Arts from 1934 to 1939. He was arrested in Slovakia on 29 April 1940 and imprisoned in Nowy Sącz and Tarnów before being sent to Auschwitz on 14 June 1940. In Auschwitz he became prisoner number 564. On 29 December 1942 he escaped from the camp. He was arrested again but was not recognized as an escapee. He was imprisoned in several camps: Auschwitz, Buchenwald, Gross-Rosen, and Dachau, from where he was liberated on 29 April 1945. He now lives in the United States.

Jerzy Adam Brandhuber (23 Oct. 1897–19 July 1981) was born in Cracow and graduated from the Academy of Fine Arts. He was arrested in 1942 and imprisoned in Jasło prison and Tarnów before being sent to Auschwitz on 14 January 1943. In Auschwitz he became prisoner number 87112. On 29 October 1944 he was transferred to Sachsenhausen. The camp was evacuated in the spring of 1945, and on 3 May he was liberated near Schwerin. At the beginning of 1947, he joined the staff of the Auschwitz–Birkenau State Museum. *Note:* Although some of Brandhuber's pictures illustrate scenes from gas chambers, he was not in fact a member of the Sonderkommando.

Bronisław Czech (25 July 1908–5 June 1944) was born in Zakopane, where he attended the Zakopane School of Timber Industry from 1925 to 1927. He was a champion skier, taking part in the Olympic Games in St Moritz in 1928, Lake Placid in 1932, and Garmisch-Partenkirchen in 1936. From 1932 to 1935 he attended the Central Institute of Physical Education, Warsaw. On 14 May 1940 he was arrested in Zakopane and imprisoned there; later he was sent to the Tarnów prison. On 14 June 1940 he was sent to Auschwitz, where he became prisoner number 349. He died in the camp four years later.

Wincenty Gawron (28 Jan. 1908–25 Aug. 1991) was born in Stara Wieś near Limanowa. He studied art in Lwów, Cracow, and Warsaw. Arrested on 18 January 1941 in Limanowa, he was sent to Auschwitz where he became prisoner number 11237. He escaped on 16 May 1942 and took part in the Warsaw uprising in 1944. After the war he moved to the United States.

Text continued on p. 257.

Mieczysław Kościelniak, *Women Prisoners Marching Out to Work* (from the 'Day of a Woman Prisoner' cycle). Pen and ink, 26 x 32 in., 1950.

[231]

Top: Władysław Siwek, *Marching Out to Work*. Water-colour, 11 x 16 in., 1946.

Bottom left: Włodzimierz Siwierski, *Regulating the Soła River*. Pencil, 4 x 6 in., 1940.

Bottom right: Włodzimierz Siwierski, *Working in Water*. Pencil, 4 x 2 in., 1940 or 1941.

Władysław Siwek, *Digging
Foundations for a New Block*.
Tempera, 44 x 60 in., 1948.

Top: Mieczysław Kościelniak,
Murder of a Prisoner at Work. Pen
and ink, 28 x 30 in., 1972.

Bottom: Wincenty Gawron,
Marching Out to Work. Pencil,
9 x 12 in., 1942.

Władysław Siwek, *Searching
Prisoners Returning from Work.*
Water-colour, 28 x 40 in., 1950.

[236]

Top left: Władysław Siwek, *A Penal Unit Returning from Work.* Oil on canvas, 30 x 80 in., 1949.

Bottom left: Mieczysław Kościelniak, *Roll-Call in Auschwitz I.* Oil, 40 x 60 in., 1972.

Bottom right: Mieczysław Kościelniak, *Evening Roll-Call at the Women's Camp.* Pen and ink, 26 x 32 in., 1950.

[237]

Top left: Władysław Siwek, *Roll-Call on Christmas Eve,* 1940. Oil, 24 x 54 in., 1948.

Bottom left: Wincenty Gawron, *During a Roll-Call.* Oil, 34 x 42 in., 1964 (from a sketch made in 1942).

Top right: Włodzimierz Siwierski, *Mealtime.* Pencil, 4 x 6 in., 1940.

Bottom right: Mieczysław Kościelniak, *Serving Out the Soup* (from the 'Day of a Woman Prisoner' cycle). Pen and ink, 26 x 32 in., 1950.

[239]

Władysław Siwek, *Scooping Up Spilt
Soup*. Water-colour, 28 x 40 in., 1950.

[240]

Mieczysław Kościelniak, *Looking After a Sick Companion*. Pen and ink, 20 x 16 in., 1946.

Mieczysław Kościelniak, *Friendship*.
Oil, 22 x 28 in., 1948.

Mieczysław Kościelniak, *Delousing*.
Pen and ink, 28 x 40 in., 1972.

[242]

Władysław Siwek, *Selection in the Bathhouse*. Water-colour, 28 x 40 in., 1950.

Francis Reisz, *Selection among the Women Prisoners*. Brush, black water-colour, 5 x 8 in., 1945.

[244]

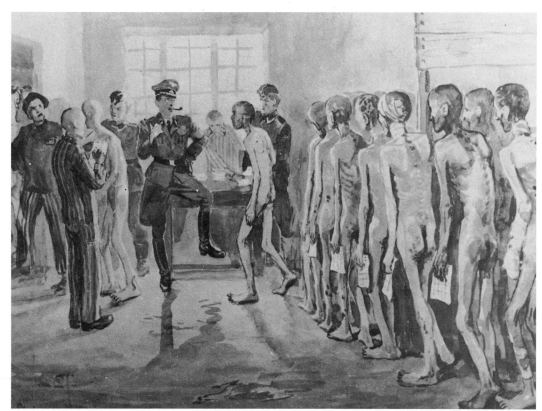

Jerzy Potrzebowski, *Selection of the Sick for the Gas Chamber*. Water-colour, 28 x 36 in., 1950.

Władysław Siwek, *A Flogging*. Water-colour, 30 x 42 in., 1948.

"SŁUPEK"

Władysław Siwek, *Hanging from Posts*. Water-colour, 12 x 16 in., 1946.

Jerzy Potrzebowski, *Prisoners in Auschwitz I Waiting to Be Taken to the Gas Chamber*. Water-colour, 36 x 48 in., 1950.

Mieczysław Kościelniak, *Making an Example of Prisoners Caught Trying to Escape*. Pen and ink, 28 x 40 in., 1972.

Francis Reisz, *Death at the Barbed Wire*. Brush, black water-colour, 6 x 8 in., 1945.

Jan Baraś-Komski, *Caught Trying to Escape*. Pen and ink, 6 x 8 in., 1945.

Jerzy Adam Brandhuber, *Killed Trying to Escape* (from the 'Auschwitz' cycle). Crayon, 14 x 22 in., 1946.

[249]

Mieczysław Kościelniak, *Carrying the Dead to the Crematorium in Auschwitz I*. Pen and ink, 28 x 40 in., 1972.

Jan Baraś-Komski, *An Execution in Auschwitz I*. Pen and ink, 6 x 8 in., 1945.

Jerzy Potrzebowski, *On the Way to
a Gas Chamber in Auschwitz II-
Birkenau*. Water-colour, 28 x 36 in.,
1950.

Władysław Siwek, *A Cart-load of
Corpses Being Dragged from the
Execution Yard in Auschwitz I*.
Water-colour, 24 x 32 in., 1950.

Top: Jerzy Adam Brandhuber,
Arrival of a Train-load of Prisoners
(from the 'Ramp' cycle). Crayon,
20 x 40 in., 1949.

Bottom: Jerzy Adam Brandhuber,
The Splitting Up of Families (from the
'Ramp' cycle). Crayon, 20 x 40 in.,
1949.

[254]

Top: Jerzy Adam Brandhuber, *Descending the Stairs Leading to the Gas Chamber* (from the 'Auschwitz' cycle). Crayon, 20 x 40 in., 1949.

Bottom: Jerzy Adam Brandhuber, *Inside the Gas Chamber* (from the 'Ramp' cycle). Crayon, 20 x 40 in., 1949.

Mieczysław Kościelniak, *Burning
Documents in January 1945*. Pen and
ink, 28 x 40 in., 1972.

[256]

Mieczysław Kościelniak (29 Jan. 1912–6 Mar. 1993) was born in Kalisz and graduated from the Cracow Academy of Fine Arts. He was sent to Auschwitz on 2 May 1941, where he became prisoner number 15261. He was evacuated to Mauthausen in January 1945 and was liberated from the Ebensee sub-camp in Austria on 6 May 1945. His paintings depict scenes from both Auschwitz and Ebensee.

Jerzy Potrzebowski (5 Sept. 1921–28 May 1974) was born in Sandomierz. He was sent to Auschwitz on 24 May 1943, where he became prisoner number 122836. In 1943 he was transferred to Buchenwald. After liberation, he studied at the Cracow Academy of Fine Arts and exhibited his work at the Bohmans Konstgaleri in Stockholm.

Francis Reisz was born in Vienna on 3 April 1909. A painter, he was arrested in Paris in July 1941 and held in the Pithiviers camp. He was sent to Auschwitz on 27 June 1942, where he became prisoner number 42447. He was evacuated to Mauthausen in January 1945 and liberated from the Ebensee sub-camp on 6 May 1945.

Władysław Siwek (14 Apr. 1907–27 Mar. 1983) was born in Niepołomice. He was arrested on 14 January 1940 and held in the Montelupich prison in Cracow; later he was imprisoned in Tarnów. He was sent to Auschwitz on 8 October 1940, where he became prisoner number 5826. He was transferred to Oranienburg on 29 October 1944. The camp was evacuated in the spring of 1945, and on 3 May he was liberated near the town of Schwerin. Subsequently, Siwek worked as an artist for the Auschwitz–Birkenau State Museum. More than fifty of his works depict life in the camp.

Włodzimierz Siwierski (19 Sept. 1905–19 Oct. 1984) was born in Chełmno and studied fine arts in Omsk and Moscow from 1918 to 1923. He was arrested in September 1940 and held in the Pawiak prison in Warsaw. He was taken to Auschwitz on 22 September 1940, where he became prisoner number 4629. He worked in the camp's workshops.

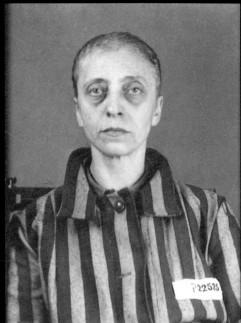

Above. Prisoner number 22535: Maria Mioduszewska, a Polish political prisoner who was brought to Auschwitz on 13 or 14 October 1942 and died there on 30 November 1942.

Opposite. Prisoner number 39655: Karol Świebocki, a Polish political prisoner, a member of the Polish underground Home Army who was brought to Auschwitz on 17 June 1942. He developed typhus and was sent to be murdered in the 'white house' (an early provisional gas chamber in Auschwitz II-Birkenau) on 10 August 1942. His son Henryk survived the war and has for many years worked as a historian at the Auschwitz Museum; he is married to Teresa Świebocka, editor of this book. (*Note:* The clothes Karol Świebocki was wearing had been those of another prisoner and still bore that prisoner's number, hence the apparent discrepancy between the photos.)

Auschwitz Today:
The Auschwitz–Birkenau
State Museum

WHEN Auschwitz was liberated on 27 January 1945 by Soviet soldiers of the 60th Army of the First Ukrainian Front, there were about 7,000 men and women still alive in the camp and a further 500 in its various sub-camps. They were completely emaciated human beings. Medical personnel of the Soviet army and local members of the Polish Red Cross offered them what medical help they could.

The Soviet army liberated the prisoners from the horrors and torments of the concentration camp, but could not liberate them from their memories. Some of the survivors determined to perpetuate the memory of those who had suffered and died, declaring that the ground saturated with their blood should be set aside as a permanent memorial to them. That same year, at a plenary meeting of the Polish National People's Council held in Warsaw on 31 December 1945, Dr Alfred Fiderkiewicz, a former prisoner of Auschwitz, moved on behalf of a group of deputies that the area of the former concentration camp in Auschwitz be officially designated a place of martyrdom. His resolution was adopted; after all, the Nazis had murdered one in five of all the citizens of pre-war Poland. Approximately half of the Polish citizens who had died were Jewish and half were ethnic Poles.

Following this resolution, on 2 July 1947 the Polish parliament resolved to preserve for all time the site of the former Auschwitz concentration camp, together with all its buildings and installations. It was declared 'a monument to the martyrdom and struggle of the Polish and other peoples', and placed under the care of the state. The resolution also provided for a state museum to be established on the site and specified its scope and responsibilities.

The Auschwitz–Birkenau State Museum was the first museum to be established on the grounds of a former Nazi concentration camp. Initially its activities were limited to the administration of the grounds and buildings in its care and the preservation of the physical fabric of the site. In 1956, the Museum's boundaries were formally defined to include a land area of 191 hectares, of which 20 hectares were in Auschwitz I and 171 hectares in Auschwitz II-Birkenau. A series of conservation zones were set up, and a long-term programme was developed for the Museum's activities in three key areas: conservation, scholarly research, and education. This programme was approved by the Polish Council for the Protection of Monuments of Struggle and Martyrdom, but it was a very ambitious plan given the financial and other constraints of that period. It was clear that achievement of these objectives was going to be a difficult task.

Over the years, the Museum has been supported by a number of official Polish bodies: the Ministry of Culture and Art, the Council for the Protection of Monuments of Struggle and Martyrdom, and the Central Commission for the Investigation of Nazi Crimes in Poland. During this time, various changes have been introduced into the Museum's programme and its operational procedures. It is fair to say that the accomplishments of the Auschwitz Museum have led to its being considered today as a model for other museums created on the sites of former Nazi concentration camps.

One major problem that the Museum had to face immediately on its establishment was that although the Polish government had declared that the buildings and installations of the former concentration camp were to be preserved for all time, parts of the original physical fabric of the camp had been radically altered before the Museum came into existence because of the Nazi attempts to destroy the evidence of their crimes when they evacuated the camp in 1945. The question for the Museum was how far it should interfere in the process of conservation. Should the appearance of the camp be kept as it had looked when the camp was operational, or as it was when it was liberated in 1945, or as it was when the Museum was established two years later, in 1947? In other words, should structures which had been ruined be reconstructed? This was the immediate dilemma that was confronted when a conservation policy for the site had to be prepared at the outset of the Museum's existence.

A striking example of the problem concerned the ruins of the gas chambers and crematoria in Auschwitz II-Birkenau. Was their original appearance to be restored? This was not a simple question: the fact that these buildings had been destroyed because the Nazis had wanted to remove all traces of their crimes is in itself part of the history of the camp. Would a reconstruction of the murder installations convey more than the ruins did? The ruins testified not only to the existence and extent of these installations, but were evidence also of the Nazi attempt to conceal the atrocities they had committed. The decision reached by the Museum was to leave the ruins in Auschwitz II-Birkenau as they were, but to restore the gas chamber and crematorium of Auschwitz I as part of a general exhibition to be housed in the former barracks alongside that would present detailed documentation of the Nazis' premeditated crimes.

The Museum's decision not to restore the original appearance of the gas chambers, crematoria, and most other structures in Auschwitz II-Birkenau was undoubtedly the right one. For example, the jury of the Auschwitz trial held in Frankfurt in the 1960s visited the site of the former murder camp several times, and on each visit were able to treat the site as constituting material evidence against the individual Nazis standing trial, and indeed against the entire Nazi murder apparatus. More recently, this approach to the conservation question was clearly a factor in the decision by Unesco to include the Auschwitz Museum in its World Heritage list.

The Museum's conservation activities have not been limited to buildings and other structures of the camp but have extended to cover all the remaining material evidence of the crimes committed at Auschwitz: for example, the piles of hair that had been cut from the heads of women murdered in the gas chambers; the rolls of haircloth made from it; and the personal and household items (shoes, spectacles, clothing, ritual objects, cooking utensils, toiletry articles, and so forth) that had been brought to Auschwitz by the unsuspecting victims in their luggage. Large quantities of all these items are carefully preserved in the Museum. The Museum also possesses works of art created by prisoners in the camp, with official sanction or clandestinely; and in addition it has a collection of works of art created by former prisoners since the liberation of the camp, as well as works created by other artists in silent homage to the more than a million people murdered in Auschwitz. Finally, it maintains a collection of memorial plaques donated by family members, groups of former prisoners, religious congregations, and others.

In order to perpetuate the memory of those who were murdered, a major monument has been erected in Auschwitz II-Birkenau, following an international competition for its design. No fewer than 400 artists, from all over the world, responded to the call for proposals.

Another aspect of the Museum's work is the detailed historical documentation of what happened at Auschwitz. The Museum is obliged by statute to collect and analyse the relevant documents and to publish its findings. As a consequence of the implementation of this policy, the Museum now holds the world's largest collection of archival materials concerning the history of Auschwitz, and also holds material on other concentration camps. Studies prepared by the Museum staff have appeared in more than 300 scholarly and popular publications; the Museum's own publications, in Polish and other languages, include the *Hefte von Auschwitz* (*Zeszyty Oświęcimskie*), memoirs, monographs, albums, catalogues, guide books, and so on. In all, the Museum has printed more than 5 million copies of texts on Auschwitz.

The Museum is also active in educating the general public, not only within the Museum itself but also through lectures and exhibitions elsewhere in Poland and abroad. Since it opened in 1947, the Museum's permanent exhibition in Auschwitz had by 1992 been seen by more than 21 million visitors, including more than 4.6 million foreigners. The average annual number of visitors in the last twenty years has been about 600,000, of whom about one-third have been foreigners. With an eye to increasing the effectiveness of the Museum's educational purpose, visitor surveys are conducted on a regular basis. Twenty-six exhibitions have been mounted abroad: in Austria, Belgium, Czechoslovakia, the Federal Republic of Germany (including West Berlin), the German Democratic Republic, Holland, Hungary, Israel, Italy, Japan, the Soviet Union, Sweden, Switzerland, the United Kingdom, the United States—at the United Nations headquarters in New York, and in many other major US cities—and Yugoslavia. These exhibitions, organized in collaboration with various foreign organizations and institutions, have been visited by several million people.

The Museum also collaborates internationally with the staff of other museums that have been established on the sites of former Nazi concentration camps: international conferences devoted to the discussion of common problems are held in Auschwitz every few years.

In declaring the Auschwitz Museum to be 'a monument to the martyrdom and struggle of the Polish and other peoples', the Polish government clearly acknowledged the international significance of the site. This was given practical expression in the Museum through the establishment of a number of national exhibitions organized by the various countries that the camp's victims had been deported from. There is also an exhibition devoted to Jewish martyrdom set up by the Museum with the help of the Jewish Historical Institute in Warsaw and other Jewish organizations.

The space available here is too short to give more than an outline of the activities of the Auschwitz Museum. Their purpose, in brief, is to remind the world of the immensity of the Nazi murder system and to warn that ideologies dedicated to spreading hatred among nations and ethnic groups lead to genocide. The Museum does this through its programmes of historical research, exhibitions, lectures, films, and publications. Its aim, far from being to foster hatred towards those who perpetrated the crimes, is to provide testimony to the truth, to warn of the consequences of war, and to foster peace in the world.

People continue to visit the Museum in large numbers: heads of state and public figures, politicians and activists, students and scholars, ordinary people—old and young—from every continent. Auschwitz survivors, now living in many different countries, also come to visit the Museum, often accompanied by their children and grandchildren. But it is a sobering thought that despite these crowds of visitors, the number coming to the Museum in any given year has always been less than the number of people the Nazis murdered in the camp.

Visitors bow their head in silence, offering their homage to the human lives reduced to ashes, to the unspeakable suffering and tragedy that took place well within the span of human memory. There is an unspoken realization that Auschwitz stands witness to what the fate of humankind will be if we are indifferent to the ideal of peace and the value of human life. The Museum will have achieved its objectives if by conveying the enormity of the crimes committed in Auschwitz it educates future generations towards the highest values of humanity: the right of all peoples to live in freedom and peace.

Kazimierz Smoleń

Previous pages: Auschwitz I. Gas Chamber and
Crematorium I (p. 265). Entrance to Auschwitz I
(p. 266–67).

Above: Inside Auschwitz I.

[268]

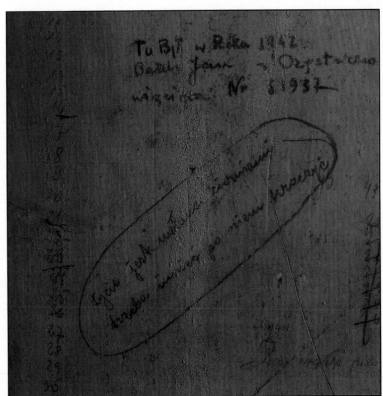

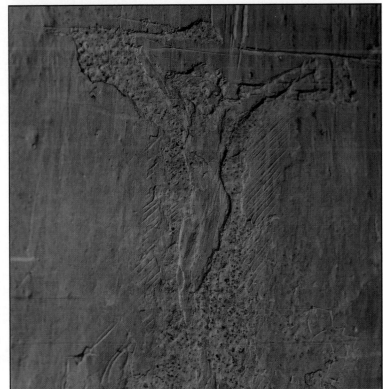

Top: Auschwitz I. An inscription made by a prisoner on the wall of cell 6 in the cellar of Block 11: 'Jan B. from Częstochowa was here in 1942, prisoner no. 31937.' The text inside the circle reads, 'Life is strewn with thorns, one must know how to get through it.'

Bottom: Auschwitz I. A crucifix carved on the wall of cell 21 in Block 11, probably by prisoner Stefan Jasieński.

Auschwitz I. The triple perimeter fence, with two watch-towers.

Auschwitz I. Inside Crematorium I.

[272]

Auschwitz II-Birkenau. Ruins of the undressing room of
Gas Chamber and Crematorium II.

Top left: Auschwitz II-Birkenau. The interior of a brick-built barrack.

Top right: Auschwitz II-Birkenau. Cutlery found on the site of the warehouses in 'Canada', where property plundered from prisoners was stored.

Bottom: Auschwitz II-Birkenau. Pond into which human ashes were dumped.

[274]

Top left: Auschwitz II-Birkenau. Watch-towers on the unloading ramp.

Top right: Auschwitz II-Birkenau. View of the main gate and guardhouse. (Photograph taken during the making of a film)

Bottom: Auschwitz II-Birkenau. View of sector BII*a* (the quarantine camp) seen from the main gate and guardhouse.

[275]

Auschwitz II-Birkenau. The papal mass held here in 1979
was attended by half a million people.

[276]

Auschwitz II-Birkenau. Jewish delegations of different
sorts come to Auschwitz from all over the world.
Some carry Israeli flags, symbol of a proud and
independent Jewish state; some wear the yellow stars that
symbolized Jewish humiliation in Nazi times.
All come to commemorate the people who were
murdered, the past that was destroyed.

Auschwitz I. Wreaths left by visitors and by the families
and friends of people shot at the Wall of Executions in the
yard of Block 11.

[278]

Auschwitz II-Birkenau. Wreaths and memorial torches
burning at the international monument erected at
the end of the railway that led directly to the gas chambers
and crematoria.

Auschwitz. On All Saints' Day (1 November), local Poles remember those murdered in Auschwitz by lighting candles in different parts of the former camp. These candles are at the Wall of Executions in the yard of Block 11 in Auschwitz I.

[280]

Personal Reflections on Auschwitz Today

What Does Auschwitz Mean Today?

The history of Auschwitz by no means came to an end when it was liberated by the Soviet army in January 1945: rather, it entered a new phase. The purpose of publishing a section of contemporary photographs in this album is to lay before the reader an image of what Auschwitz looks like today. This image needs to be considered in its own right and also as an introduction to the question of what Auschwitz actually means today.

People who have never visited Auschwitz probably imagine that the place has crumbled into the dust, that there is nothing left there to see today. At best, perhaps, they might imagine a large open field, with tall grasses swaying in the wind, and in season a sprinkling of blood-red poppies—something like the well-known television images of First World War battlefields in Belgium, for example.

In fact, this is not the case: there is still a physical Auschwitz, though much of it is in ruins. And that physical Auschwitz lingers on, a haunting symbol that the inhumanity it represents is also part of the real world today.

The continued existence of Auschwitz is an accident of history. Other Nazi murder camps, such as those at Treblinka, Bełżec, or Sobibór, were deliberately dynamited by the SS before the war was over in order to conceal the incriminating evidence. They intended to do likewise at Auschwitz, and began by blowing up the gas chambers at Auschwitz II-Birkenau, but because of the speed of the advance of the Soviet army the job was never finished. Much of the physical fabric of Auschwitz thus survived the war—not only the ruins of the gas chambers and the crematoria, but also the barracks, the watch-towers, the barbed-wire fences, the railway line that led nowhere except to the gas chambers.

The Polish parliament declared the site a national monument and set up a museum administration to preserve the remains, of which today there are at least 150 buildings and 250 ruins. Many of the barracks were converted to house photographic displays and exhibitions. Terrifying original artefacts, such as the tresses of hair cut off the heads of murdered women, were put on display behind glass, as were thousands of suitcases, pots and pans, spectacles and false limbs that had belonged to the murder victims. Conservation works were undertaken; a major programme of historical research was instituted; a library and archive were established.

Over the years Auschwitz has attracted huge numbers of visitors—tourists, pilgrims, even Auschwitz survivors themselves. The visit to Auschwitz became a statutory part of educating Polish schoolchildren. Visitors now number about half a million per year; since the war was over in 1945 as many as twenty million people have been to Auschwitz as visitors.

As for the Museum, it has become a major enterprise, employing nearly 200 people: they work in administration, conservation, education, publishing, research and acquisitions, and in the archives; there are guides, cleaners, accountants. Within the site there is a guest house, a cafeteria, a souvenir shop, several bookshops, a cinema auditorium with its own ticket office, a post office, a currency exchange office, a tea room, a left-luggage office, a series of public lavatories—all the paraphernalia associated with mass tourism, although entrance to the museum itself is free of charge.

So Auschwitz survived the war: but what does its survival actually mean? The difficulty is that it means many different things at the same time. Auschwitz is, as we have seen, a museum, a place that tourists come to, on their own or in guided tours. But Auschwitz is also one vast cemetery, a place of pilgrimage, where people come to lay flowers, light candles, say their prayers, observe their silences—at the ruins of the gas chambers, at the fields where human ashes were dumped, at the wall of executions, at the large international monument that has been erected. In fact, the totality of Auschwitz is a monument to itself. We don't have a word in our language adequately to describe what this place is.

But if the survival of Auschwitz was originally an accident of history, its continued survival to this day has been the result of conscious political decisions by the authorities. It is necessary to recognize, therefore, that an important part of its meaning derives from the particular social and political setting of postwar Poland. For more than forty years the Polish Communist government emphasized its national and educational significance on at least two levels: the evils of Nazi Fascism, and the crimes committed by the wartime occupiers against Polish society and Polish culture. Auschwitz was made to symbolize for Poles the rape and mutilation of their country by the Germans: at least 75,000 ethnic Poles met their deaths in this place. Western visitors to Auschwitz, particularly Jews, have expressed surprise—and have been not a little offended—that although 90 per cent of those who were murdered in Auschwitz were Jews, the Museum paid scant attention to this in its exhibitions. Nearly forty-five years went by after the end of the war with the mass murder of Jews hardly being publicly mentioned in the Auschwitz Museum, and certainly it was not given appropriate prominence. It was as if Auschwitz had abandoned the memory of the Jews. It stood for other memories, other meanings.

The situation changed dramatically after 1989. With the fall of Communist government in that year, the country set about a transition to democracy, and one of its first and critical tasks was to encourage greater understanding of political and cultural pluralism. In the last years of Communist government, Auschwitz was the setting for an exceptionally bitter conflict between Poles and Jews, occasioned by the establishment of a Carmelite convent in a building that had been used partly to store Zyklon B. The strength of Western Jewish opposition to the convent (still continuing at the time of writing) demonstrates that the physical Auschwitz today deeply matters to people, and that, even so long after the end of the war, care must be exercised to express the right meanings for the place, to preserve Auschwitz in a manner fitting to the memory of those who died there.

With the new pluralist mood in Poland today, a reappraisal of the meanings of Auschwitz is high on the agenda, but to find a way of doing this in a manner that will satisfy everyone is by no means an easy task. One of the first steps was made in 1989, when the first post-Communist government set up an International Council for the Museum, which included representatives of the Jewish and Gypsy communities. Among many other recommendations, the Council endorsed the closure of at least two of the exhibitions set up by countries of the former Soviet bloc that merely promoted Communist ideology without paying proper heed to meanings of Auschwitz that ought to have been stated.

But what are those meanings? Who are the experts who can say for sure what Auschwitz means, or what it ought to mean? Indeed, who is Auschwitz for? The victims, the survivors, ourselves? Or are we all to consider ourselves as victims, all Auschwitz survivors in some sense or another? The historians and survivors can tell us *what* happened at Auschwitz, but sociologists and theologians have yet to explain adequately *why* Auschwitz happened at all. We are left only with the questions and incomplete answers.

We who live after the liberation of Auschwitz will continue to debate long into the future how best to deal with its universal moral lessons and significance, while at the same time finding ways adequately to lament the specific individuals and communities destroyed during the war, and to identify the kinds of people who were the murderers.

Auschwitz: A Symbol of What?

It is common enough for people to say that Auschwitz is a symbol, but for different people

Auschwitz is a symbol of different things. For Jews, Auschwitz is the symbol of the Holocaust—*the* symbol of the Holocaust, and symbolizing only the Holocaust. For Poles, Auschwitz is the symbol of the Nazi oppression of Poland. For Gypsies, Auschwitz symbolizes the Nazi genocide of their people. Members of other minority groups, such as Jehovah's Witnesses or homosexuals, also suffered and died in Auschwitz—the ultimate consequence of total social rejection. And then there are those for whom Auschwitz is less a symbol of the persecution and obliteration of particular groups or nations but rather of more universalist issues—for example, the death of God, the end of classical European civilization, the intrinsic flaws in human nature or in modern bureaucratic society that brought such evil into the world and is still doing so. Nor should it be overlooked that Auschwitz is a part of modern German history—whether as a symbol of something best forgotten or, on the contrary, a symbol of an aspect of German-ness that will linger on to haunt future generations.

There is nothing particularly improper about Auschwitz having more than one set of meanings. Different people are interested in different things. It is quite normal for different ethnic groups to have different histories and to see the same event in different ways, selecting and symbolizing the relevant facts that are important for them. For Poles, the historical fact that the first train-load of deportees to Auschwitz consisted of Polish political prisoners has considerable symbolic importance. Jews, on the other hand, would scarcely be aware of this historical fact, let alone the fact that nearly two more years elapsed before the first transports of Jews arrived at Auschwitz. Such facts are of no relevance to those who see Auschwitz in the context not of Polish history but of Jewish history—whether (for example) as a symbol of the total powerlessness of diaspora Judaism, or as a symbol of the ultimate Jewish sacrifice the purpose of which was to lay the way for a divine redemption that manifested itself shortly afterwards in the establishment of the state of Israel. Not all facts about Auschwitz possess the same intrinsic importance to everyone; facts are selected according to the nature of the particular symbols that people identify themselves with.

It has to be said that not all the Nazi concentration camps live on in the popular mind as symbols. Bełżec, a camp in eastern Poland where the Nazis murdered 600,000 Jews, has been almost completely forgotten in the West, and even by Jews—probably because there were almost no survivors (unlike the case of Auschwitz), and because nothing at all of the camp physically survived (again, unlike Auschwitz). Jews did not protest when a Carmelite convent was established at Dachau, probably because there were no gas chambers in Dachau, with the result that Dachau did not become a Jewish symbol of the Holocaust.

The historical memory is selective; it does not and cannot recall everything. This is what thinking in symbols, or thinking with symbols, is about: to treat part of the history as representative of the whole, to shrink it down to something of a manageable size. Too much happened in Auschwitz for people to remember it all: the gas chambers, the crematoria, the slow deaths and punitive regime in the concentration camp, the steady dehumanization of the living, the remarkable linguistic and cultural diversity of its inhabitants and victims, and indeed the extraordinary scale of it all. Thinking in symbols is not a rational or logical mode of thought; but symbols are there for people to believe in, they are there to summarize the key things that are of importance to them. Even the term 'Holocaust' is itself a symbol in this sense—it summarizes and condenses within a single term the enormous and complex process, in many different countries and circumstances, by which six million Jewish lives were brought to nothing. By definition, then, the use of symbols often means that people do not necessarily know precise, detailed answers to normal, logical questions: When did the Holocaust begin? When did it end? Where did it happen? Why did it happen? The whole point about a symbol is that it allows one to possess cultural knowledge without having the totality of the facts. And this in turn is why the physical encounter with Auschwitz today can be a fundamentally disorienting experience: one is brought face to face with other facts, other symbols, about which one may have previously been quite unaware.

Things Look Different when Seen Close Up

One of the curious by-products of symbolic modes of thought about Auschwitz is that people often think they know all about it even before they have even been there. Many people have told me that they have no need to visit Auschwitz; they say that they can perfectly well 'remember' Auschwitz and its lessons without physically coming face to face with it. Maybe they are simply afraid to go.

It is one thing to think about Auschwitz from the comfortable distance of London, New York, or Canberra. It is quite another to do so in Auschwitz. Contemporary problems of race relations—'ethnic cleansing', for example—let alone the atrocities of the Second World War in Europe look quite different when viewed from the perspective of a watch-tower above the vast bleakness of Auschwitz II-Birkenau. Perhaps the first impression that visitors to Auschwitz usually receive is the sudden awareness that their symbols indeed derive from concrete realities: Auschwitz really existed, the mass murders really happened, and they happened in this actual place. Standing inside the gas chamber, touching the crematorium door, walking along the corridors of the underground prison cells, silently contemplating the bleak open expanse of Auschwitz II-Birkenau with its barbed-wire fences and watch-towers—all these sensations bring home the realities experienced by Auschwitz victims and the unabated terror of other victims in other places still today.

But the visitor's experience is more than just the process of mentally re-enacting the historical nightmares or of filling out the details. More significant, perhaps, is the developing awareness that one's well-worn slogans express little more than simplistic myths about Auschwitz and are woefully inadequate to convey the truth of its sheer size and complexity. Such slogans as 'Remember!', 'Never Again', or 'No More War!' may satisfy the conscience, but they scarcely even begin to create a personal relationship with the actual details of the horrors. Of course, it would be an exaggeration to claim that any visit to Auschwitz will always stir the emotions—yet it is likely that for the ordinary person the direct encounter with the physical place, the opportunity to touch history, will provoke a deeper understanding. One of the things that a deeper understanding may well lead to is the adjustment of preconceptions based on popular stereotypes—notably, about the kind of person who became an Auschwitz victim. After all, there were many different kinds of people who suffered and died at Auschwitz—for example, many different kinds of Jews (including atheists, deeply religious Jews, Communists, and converts to Christianity), many different kinds of Poles (including members of the intelligentsia, priests, Communists, ordinary people arrested during round-ups, and those who had helped Jews). The encounter with the place exposes visitors to details like this which collectively can help to reshape their concept of Auschwitz and what happened there. The physical sight of the ruins of the gas chambers and crematoria within their barbed-wire compounds may also force the onlooker to reconsider some of the moral dimensions—for example, the popular dismissive image of Jews 'going like sheep to the slaughter' may develop into an empathy with those terrified and disoriented human beings about to be murdered in a harmless-looking shower-room.

It does need to be said, however, that the direct encounter with Auschwitz can actually have a reverse effect. Indeed, there are many things which the visitor may somehow find inappropriate. Those making their first visit to the site of a former concentration camp might expect something totally disordered, shapeless, threatening; but what they see instead at Auschwitz I is a solid set of military barracks arranged neatly in rows, separated by well-maintained avenues and landscaped with tall trees and grass verges set correctly within kerbstone borders. The crowds of tourists thronging the exhibitions on a hot summer's day, or the welter of detailed historical information proffered by the guides, can disrupt a sense of profound sadness or moral loneliness which might otherwise have dominated the mood of the visitor. One may actually be distracted from comprehending the meaning of the place by the sheer banality of the surviving artefacts—as if what Auschwitz is about can be reduced to the watch-towers, the barbed-wire fences, the display cases of shoes or spectacles. Walking to the gas chambers in Auschwitz today is in no sense the same as walking to the gas chambers in Auschwitz then; but for the visitor the temptation remains to confuse the ruins that are to be seen with the realities of their past. So would it not in the end be better if there were nothing at all to see, merely a wide open field with tall grasses swaying in the wind? How would one's understanding of Auschwitz be affected if this were the case?

Putting the question in this way provokes the thought that even the physical Auschwitz as it is today is but a symbol of its past. There are no surviving artefacts at Treblinka, Bełżec, or Sobibór, although at Treblinka an especially striking monument, consisting principally of a valley of rough stones, has been erected on the site. Here it is the monument, rather than the surviving artefacts, that captures the imagination and in some sense distracts the mind away from the realities they represent.

The problem, in short, is that in order to grasp the enormity of the place, what is needed is a way of learning how to see and how to interpret what one is looking at— in other words, a philosophy of sight-seeing. It is no good saying that there is no purpose in going to Auschwitz because the mind will be distracted by the ruins of the apparatus of mass murder, that there is no point in going to Treblinka because it will be hard to contemplate the evil of the place in a setting where there is nothing to see except a monument in a picturesque meadow. But does a tombstone in an ordinary cemetery explain the meaning of life, or of death? It is certainly true that to see Auschwitz close-up is not at all straightforward. On the contrary, the visitor may well refuse to absorb the manifold messages of the sight-seeing experience in Auschwitz and reject as irrelevant any information—imparted by the guide, for instance—which disturbs his or her pre-existing symbolic knowledge. For people in such a mood, sight-seeing is a powerful way of reinforcing an existing opinion, and they tend to pick out what they already know. But then, on the way home, they may begin to feel that what they learned in Auschwitz can indeed be carried back with them: that Auschwitz has nothing to do with any physical sense of place, for what is important about Auschwitz is ultimately what it symbolizes. The symbol that became concrete during their visit becomes once again a symbol, though now rendered more potent, and perhaps having acquired fresh meanings, through their contact with the reality of the place.

It is difficult to develop an approach to sight-seeing in Auschwitz which can truly take the visitor into new domains of personal experience. Time is usually short; the place is crowded with people, and yet there is no one to ask; one is alone with one's questions, thoughts, and emotions. There is no clear-cut formula that will enable visitors to connect their total visual experience in Auschwitz with the narrow constraints of their pre-existing symbolic knowledge. The fact is, however, that the visitor, by having come at all, has made an act of commemoration, and in so doing has affirmed a universal human gesture. The visit to the site of massacre at Auschwitz confirms the link between ourselves and those who died there—as members of particular national or ethnic groups, or simply as human beings.

Just as the survival of Auschwitz today raises questions about the ways in which we relate to the past, so too it is not self-evident how the Holocaust is to be understood today.

Some people feel that they know 'enough' about the Holocaust, and have no particular need to hear about it further. Others, while not necessarily disputing its uniqueness, would prefer to think of it as part of something bigger, such as the wider issue of ethnic intolerance or persecution in many other parts of the world. Such people feel that the meaning of Auschwitz, as in some sense the epicentre of the Holocaust, has a continuing importance for all. It is true that the murders committed at Auschwitz were conducted on a far larger scale and in a more systematic manner than anywhere else. On the other hand, to treat Auschwitz as the symbol of the Holocaust obscures the historical fact that not more than one-quarter of all the Jews murdered in the Holocaust were murdered there. It needs to be recalled that the Holocaust was not 'an event': massacres of Jews by the Nazis during the Second World War took place in all kinds of places apart from the well-known murder camps—in forests, in the streets and market squares of small towns, in gravel pits, inside synagogues, in Jewish cemeteries. As a symbol of the Holocaust, then, Auschwitz is historically very misleading.

Just as an understanding of the physical Auschwitz today can be deepened by contrasting it with the sites of those other camps where no original artefacts have survived, so too a historical understanding of the Holocaust can be deepened by a more detailed knowledge of these other murder locations in villages and forests across eastern Europe. By concentrating on Auschwitz alone one misses not only the local massacres but the whole background of the round-ups and the deportations in their local settings, the reactions of the local population, and the whole complex political interplay of ethnicity, nationalism, and Communism that characterized eastern Europe during the war—first under German and Soviet occupation, and then, after 1941, in the Soviet Union and in the other territories captured by the Germans from their Soviet occupiers. Auschwitz was a murder factory, a place of genocide whose victims had been torn from their social and moral environments, deprived of their homes and families—and their humanity. Auschwitz was in that sense a deliberate decontextualization by the Nazis.

The point is an important one because much of the postwar history of eastern Europe has been bound up with these preoccupations: the imposition of Communism after the defeat of Nazi Germany, and recently today, after the fall of Communism, by the reassertion of nationalist and ethnic identities in the newly independent countries of the former Soviet bloc. The Holocaust as such was given little public attention in most of eastern Europe during this time, and even today far less is known about it in eastern Europe than in the West. The future content of the Auschwitz symbol in eastern Europe cannot be taken for granted. Hitherto, Auschwitz has stood as an official state symbol, reinforced by the official Communist history that four million people were murdered there. This figure was a deliberate inflation—presumably in order to conceal the location of other deportations and mass murders carried out by Stalinist forces. But now for the first time, in the freer atmosphere of historical research in the new eastern Europe, it has become possible to examine what really happened during the war: some of the wartime mass graves of Poles are being dug up in the former Soviet Union, the Auschwitz figures have been revised drastically downwards (to somewhere between 1.1 and 1.5 million), and Auschwitz is beginning to return to its true identity. The view of Franciszek Piper, the head of the historical research department at the Auschwitz–Birkenau State Museum, is now that about 1 million Jews died in Auschwitz, corresponding to 90 per cent of the total number of victims; of the rest, at least 75,000 were ethnic Poles, almost 21,000 were Gypsies, about 15,000 were Soviet prisoners of war, and between 10,000 and 15,000 were people of other nationalities. The identity and the exact numbers of all the victims will probably never be known for sure; still today they are the subject of some disagreement, even among leading professional historians. What is more certain, however, is that once the truth is out in eastern Europe that Jews constituted 90 per cent of Auschwitz victims, some restructuring of Auschwitz symbolism there is bound to follow.

In Auschwitz itself, much has been happening as a reflection of these trends. The inscriptions on the main international monument at Auschwitz II-Birkenau, erected in 1967, have been removed, and new texts—which will among other things include the word 'Jew' for the first time—have been agreed. The German organization Aktion Sühnezeichen (Action Reconciliation), which since the early 1970s has been sending groups of students and teachers to Auschwitz, has built an international youth centre not far from the Museum, where for a few years now it has been hosting student seminars and study visits. A similar programme has been prepared for the new Centre for Information, Encounter, Dialogue, Education, and Prayer in Auschwitz, sponsored by the Catholic Church of Poland. These are encouraging signs of the attempt to break out from the suffocating impact of negative stereotypes (on all sides) which have dogged Polish–Jewish and Polish–German relations for many decades. Poles today are beginning to speak about their sense of a shared history with the Jews of their country—that Polish Jewish history is indeed part of Polish history; local Jewish history is beginning to be taught as part of the school curriculum, and is beginning to figure in local museums. Western Jews, for their part, are arriving in Poland in increasing numbers to visit both Auschwitz and also their places of origin. As the generation of Holocaust survivors is now dying out, there is a new Jewish sense of urgency to videotape survivors' testimonies, even on the actual site of their traumas. Jewish youth organizations have begun to send large delegations to visit Auschwitz (the biennial 'March of the Living', for example, which began in 1988). The period from 1989 to 1995 is conveniently lending itself to a wide range of fiftieth-anniversary commemorations, such as the erection of plaques at sites of martyrdom, gatherings of survivors and their children for prayer meetings, and even (to cite one remarkable case) the arranging of a special train journey from Paris to Auschwitz to re-enact symbolically the deportation of the Jews of France. The Holocaust is slowly beginning to find its mode of commemoration on the actual sites themselves, and Auschwitz is part of this process.

This trend is only part of the picture, however. Israel has for many years had its own Holocaust memorial in Jerusalem (Yad Vashem); and in the United States the current desire to erect a series of Holocaust museums, notably the major new initiative in Washington D.C., suggests that (at least in the minds of many Western Jews) Auschwitz is by no means the only appropriate location for Holocaust commemoration. On the contrary, the range and scope of memorializations has continued to increase in recent years in many countries around the world. In addition to the important work undertaken by international organizations of Holocaust survivors since the end of the war, one can point to the steady increase in memoirs and reminiscences, novels, plays, films, television documentaries, international conferences, and scholarly publications about the Holocaust. Once again, therefore, Auschwitz today is best understood in context—in terms of its emerging involvement in a wide variety of international commemorative activities.

Furthermore, in order to fulfil its educational objectives, the Auschwitz State Museum has developed strong collaborative links with Holocaust museums outside Poland. This has even meant the loan or transfer of original artefacts from Auschwitz—a development that conservationists and others may view with alarm but which has been undertaken for the purpose of contributing to the wider spread of knowledge about the Holocaust in countries far removed from the scene of the crimes, and to the benefit of those who cannot make the journey to Auschwitz.

The Holocaust today is in some senses an expanding category, both in terms of the identity of its victims (now often taken to mean all victims of Nazism, not only the Jews), and also in terms of the far wider range of events and locations in addition to Auschwitz that people are becoming increasingly aware of. The contemporary Western fascination with the Holocaust will undoubtedly mean a new role and pose a new set of questions—museological, educational, and philosophical—for the Auschwitz Museum in the years ahead.

The Auschwitz State Museum Today

Visitors who are critical of what they see at the Auschwitz State Museum should remember that the principal structure of the museum's exhibitions was designed nearly forty years ago, at a time when the great majority of the visitors consisted of Poles who had lived through the Nazi occupation. The main purpose of the Museum at that time, as an institution funded by a Communist state, was to provide as full a documentation as possible of the crimes of Nazi Fascism. Today the visitors have changed, no less than the political circumstances. With the increasing distance of time separating us from the events, more historical information needs to be provided, and from different perspectives. Moreover, people today expect modern graphics and design, even interactive exhibits. In this respect Auschwitz has the air of being provincial and old-fashioned. The Museum staff would certainly like to change both the content and form of the exhibitions, but budgetary constraints have so far prevented them from making more than marginal changes, or closing exhibitions now deemed unsuitable. So the exhibitions today are by no means a reflection of the extraordinary level of personal commitment and devotion of the staff who work there and who have to face the horror of the place every day of their working lives. It is largely because of this level of commitment by the staff (who include Auschwitz survivors themselves, children of survivors, and children of victims), supported by the newly established International Council, that there has already been a considerable amount of progress behind the scenes in considering the changes necessary to bring Auschwitz into the twenty-first century.

The question is, however, what sort of changes should be introduced? Some of the issues are relatively straightforward: for example, to create new exhibits showing the role of Auschwitz in the Holocaust; to illustrate the attitudes and behaviour of prisoners in the camp, including the human dignity that showed through in the resistance to the Nazis (whether of a spiritual, political, religious, or military nature); to say more about the identity of the victims (their culture and way of life, their social origins), even to list their names as far as possible; to explain why people were brought to Auschwitz to be murdered. The exhibitions will thus aim to tell more than they did during the Communist period.

But should today's rewriting of the wartime history of Auschwitz stress the universal human issues, or rather present the hitherto suppressed nationalist approaches to the subject? Eastern Europe may well have a different agenda in this respect from what Westerners would prefer to see: because of the numerous border changes during the course of the twentieth century, it is not even clear (for example) who is a Hungarian, who is a Pole, who is a member of a minority community. Are Polish Jews 'Jews', or are they 'Poles'? Since part of what actually happened at Auschwitz was the result of the deliberate distortion by the Nazis of the social identities of their victims, it would be tendentious to reproduce these without comment in the new exhibitions; on the other hand, not to do so (for the sake of clarity) would conceal the historical truth about Auschwitz.

In describing Auschwitz, then, whose world should the Museum be attempting to describe? The world as seen by the victims, or the world as seen by their murderers? Nazi documents and photographs ironically provide the most reliable source for depicting the objective historical truth about Auschwitz, but at the same time room has to be found for the very different, subjective evidence of prisoners—from the memoirs of survivors, for example. Finding the right balance here is not easy.

It is, furthermore, a mammoth task to create exhibitions that would fully encompass the social and political circumstances of each country whose citizens died in Auschwitz, particularly given the fact that there is a substantial imbalance of knowledge between different kinds of visitors. The imbalance is based not only on the different Auschwitz symbolisms the visitors arrive with but also on other, overlapping factors influencing their knowledge and understanding of the subject: for example, whether they are eastern or western Europeans; whether they are Jews or non-Jews; whether or not they come from countries which experienced Nazi occupation—indeed, whether or not they have a personal connection with Auschwitz, as survivors or as relatives of survivors or victims. One-third of the Museum's visitors are young people under thirty; one-third (not the same third) are foreigners, of whom a very substantial portion are from Germany. How does one construct an exhibition that will cater successfully to Israeli and Polish Catholic teenagers, to middle-aged Germans as well as elderly Frenchmen? The challenge to the Museum here is immense.

No less daunting is the problem of conservation and the continued massive physical decay of the site. Shortly after the war was over, some of the wooden barracks were dismantled; people then had no idea that future generations would deem them to have interfered with structures that possessed intrinsic historical, scientific, even theological significance. Our own obsession today with the original and the authentic is almost at the other extreme: there is something surreal about wishing to preserve in Auschwitz artefacts that stood for the notion of total destruction. Be that as it may, the Museum has done a great deal of work to conserve Auschwitz: certain features, such as the barbed-wire fences, the railway tracks, even many of the wooden watch-towers and barracks, have in fact been so heavily restored over the past forty years that they cannot be correctly described today as fully authentic.

Should such work continue to be done indefinitely? What if nothing were done? Would it be best to let the site age with the passage of time, until, at some point in the future, Auschwitz physically disappears into the ground? Or should certain authentic ruins—the ruins of the gas chambers and crematoria, for example—be treated none the less as structures worth preserving? But then how should they be preserved? Would we really want to construct a glass dome over them, with a viewing platform reached by an outside staircase? Is this what future generations would really expect us today to do with Auschwitz? Leaving aside the differences of professional opinion among conservationists on what is technically feasible (given the almost total absence of experience in such matters), and leaving aside the enormous costs of such operations (not a small issue in itself), the fundamental question remains: what should and what should not be done at Auschwitz? How far would the symbolic values of Auschwitz be affected in the future by the conservation decisions taken? The way forward is by no means self-evident.

Conclusion

Some might say, in response to such questions, that Auschwitz is its own monument; history should take its course; we should not intervene; a correct attitude to Auschwitz should be based on an ultimate silence. It is probably the most dignified approach, but is it practical?

One solution to this could be that Auschwitz—or at least certain designated parts thereof—should develop more of the character of a cemetery than it has at present, and include more monuments: a specifically Jewish monument, for example, of which there is none at

Auschwitz. For the longer-term future, one could envisage a situation in which Auschwitz would become just one of many important sites in southern Poland bearing testimony to a cruel twentieth-century history of the persecution of minorities, and in particular of the Jews.

For Auschwitz is only a part of the Jewish experience of Poland. The remaining testimony of Jewish culture in Poland is quite varied today: in the thousands of towns and villages across Poland, where a total of over three million Jews were living in September 1939, there are many synagogues and cemeteries still standing. Some of these cemeteries are still almost intact, never having been seriously damaged by the Nazis; some have been fully restored; some have disappeared completely and have been built over; some remain simply as totally empty fields, or perhaps with just one tombstone left. As for the few surviving synagogue buildings, some have been converted for other uses (usually as art galleries or public libraries), some have been fully restored, and there are some which still stand in ruins. The latter are probably the most expressive of the Holocaust, bearing silent witness to a destroyed world.

Amidst these very different kinds of testimony to the past, future generations will need to develop their own philosophy of sight-seeing, to piece together these varied sights into a coherent pattern of the meanings and symbols they will then believe in. For some, Auschwitz will be one part of this total picture; for others, Auschwitz will remain unique—the most expressive and terrifying reminder of Europe's disappeared populations.

This essay has returned several times to the fact that in the final analysis we are left only with questions and incomplete answers. To turn the well-known Nazi phrase on its head: there can be no 'final solution' for what should be done today at Auschwitz. What matters more is the need for a sense of debate, to roll back the taboos surrounding discussion of the mass murders in the heart of the continent, and to grope some way forward in this darkened terrain. There is no 'happy ending'; no fabricated consolations are appropriate in Auschwitz. The human capacity for intolerance, prejudice, and cruelty has not disappeared, even from Europe today; and in that sense the significance of Auschwitz is perennial.

The photographs in this volume that show what Auschwitz looks like today can therefore be no more than symbolic; it is impossible, in a brief selection of pictures, to do justice to the many-sided nature of the problems discussed in this essay. Every corner of Auschwitz, whether in bright sunlight or covered in low mist, raises new thoughts, new questions. Auschwitz has had a long and tortuous history since 1945; the future of Auschwitz promises to be no less challenging.

Jonathan Webber

Notes on Sources of Principal Texts Quoted

PERY BROAD, *Reminiscences*. Original manuscript in the archives of the Auschwitz–Birkenau State Museum; translated into English by Krystyna Michalik.

Pery Broad was born in Rio de Janeiro in 1921, the son of a Brazilian merchant and a German woman. Whilst still a schoolboy he returned to Germany with his mother; in 1941, at the age of 20, he volunteered for the SS. In the following year he was sent to serve in Auschwitz to work in the Political Section, where he remained, with the rank of *SS-Unterscharführer* (corporal), until the camp was liberated. He was arrested by the British, to whom he handed over a manuscript of his reminiscences about Auschwitz. He was put on trial in Frankfurt; despite a strong suspicion that he had been personally involved in the torture or murder of prisoners, formal evidence was lacking, and he was sentenced in 1965 to a term of four years' imprisonment. As of early 1993, he was known to be living in Germany, in a small town in North Rhine–Westphalia.

Broad's *Reminiscences* were published by the Museum in English translation in 1972 in a collective work entitled *KL Auschwitz Seen by the SS: Rudolf Höss, Pery Broad, Johann Paul Kremer*.

ZALMEN GRADOWSKI. Untitled original manuscript in Yiddish in the archives of the Auschwitz–Birkenau State Museum; translated into English by Krystyna Michalik, from an original translation into Polish by Bernard Mark.

Zalmen Gradowski was a Polish Jew, born in 1908 or 1909 in Suwałki near Grodno. He and his family were arrested by the Nazis in November 1942, and were deported to Auschwitz in January 1943. He lost his entire family on arrival, when his wife, mother, two sisters, father-in-law, and brother-in-law were selected for the gas chambers; Gradowski himself was ordered to become a member of the Sonderkommando. He managed to keep a detailed diary of his deportation and experiences in the camp and bury it in an aluminium flask in the vicinity of Gas Chamber and Crematorium II; over eighty pages were recovered when it was discovered in March 1945, thanks to the efforts of a fellow-prisoner who had survived and knew where Gradowski had buried it. Gradowski himself did not survive the war and probably died during the revolt of the Sonderkommando in October 1944. Those parts of his diary dealing with the time he spent in Auschwitz were published by the Museum in English translation in 1973 in a collective work entitled *Amidst a Nightmare of Crime: Manuscripts Found in Auschwitz of Prisoners in the Sonderkommando*.

RUDOLF HÖSS, *Autobiography*. Original manuscript in German in the archives of the Auschwitz–Birkenau State Museum; the excerpts cited in this volume were translated into English by Annette Winkelmann.

Rudolf Höss was born in 1900 and joined the SS in 1934. He served in Dachau and Sachsenhausen before becoming commandant of Auschwitz in May 1940. He held this post until November 1943, when he was transferred to Berlin to the Inspectorate of Concentration Camps, although he returned to Auschwitz in 1944 to supervise the mass murder of Jews deported from Hungary. When the war was over he worked as a farmer under an assumed name in the British zone of Germany, but in February 1946 he was recognized. Imprisoned in Nuremberg, he acted as a witness at the war crimes trials and was then extradited to Poland, where he was put on trial and sentenced to death. Höss was hanged in Auschwitz in April 1947.

Höss wrote his autobiography while in prison in Poland awaiting trial. Those parts of his text dealing with Auschwitz-related matters were published by the Museum in English translation in 1972 in a collective work entitled *KL Auschwitz Seen by the SS: Rudolf Höss, Pery Broad, Johann Paul Kremer.*

Supplementary Captions

Front endpapers. Children showing their prisoner numbers. (Photo taken from the Soviet film *Chronicle of the Liberation of Auschwitz,* 1945)

Pages 2–3. Mass grave in Auschwitz II-Birkenau photographed by the Soviet army after the liberation of the camp. (Photo taken from the Soviet film *Chronicle of the Liberation of Auschwitz,* 1945)

Page 4. A window of a cell in the Block of Death with a prisoner number scratched in the plaster. (Photo by Wiesław Zieliński)

Back endpapers. Auschwitz I. Some of the 600 children and young people under the age of 18 found alive in Auschwitz when the camp was liberated. (Photo taken from the Soviet film *Chronicle of the Liberation of Auschwitz,* 1945)

Notes on Contributors

RENATA BOGUSŁAWSKA-ŚWIEBOCKA was a Senior Curator of the Auschwitz–Birkenau State Museum, having studied both history and museology at the Jagiellonian University in Cracow, and curator of several exhibitions about the history of Auschwitz. She died in 1983.

KAZIMIERZ SMOLEŃ was the Director of the Auschwitz–Birkenau State Museum from 1955 to 1990. His first association with Auschwitz, though, was as a political prisoner: he spent four and a half years there as prisoner number 1327. After the camp was liberated he studied law at the Catholic University of Lublin. He gave evidence at numerous war trials and has published widely on Auschwitz.

TERESA ŚWIEBOCKA has worked in the Auschwitz–Birkenau State Museum since 1967. Today she is a Senior Curator and head of its publishing department, having studied both history and museology at the Jagiellonian University in Cracow. She is the author of several articles and other publications on the history of Auschwitz and was also responsible for putting together a number of major travelling exhibitions about Auschwitz, including those mounted in the United Nations headquarters in New York, and in many other cities in the United States and in the United Kingdom. She is currently co-director of the first complete overhaul of the Museum's general exhibition since 1956.

JONATHAN WEBBER is Fellow in Jewish Social Studies at the Oxford Centre for Postgraduate Hebrew Studies, and Hebrew Centre Lecturer in Social Anthropology at Oxford University. Since 1988 he has been conducting research on Auschwitz as it is today, and in 1990 became a founder member of the International Council of the Auschwitz–Birkenau

State Museum and chairman of its standing committee on education. He organized landmark international symposia of Jewish intellectuals on 'The Future of Auschwitz' in Yarnton, England (1990) and Cracow, Poland (1992). He is currently director of a Tempus project, funded by the European Commission in Brussels, designed to achieve co-operation between Britain and Germany in updating the Auschwitz Museum and improving Polish higher education in Jewish studies and in the understanding of ethnic issues.

CONNIE WILSACK lives in Oxford and is Managing Editor of the Littman Library of Jewish Civilization. She has edited some fifty books, in a variety of scholarly fields.

Technical Credits

Editorial board: Włodzimierz Gałąska, Krzysztof Krempa, Bronisław Migdalski, Franciszek Piper, Tomislav Rakočević, Teresa Świebocka, Jonathan Webber, Connie Wilsack

Graphic design: Rade Rančič

Documentary photographs: Archives of the Auschwitz–Birkenau State Museum

Colour photographs: Wiesław Zieliński, except for photos on p. 276 (Andrzej Kosobudzki) and p. 277 (Jerzy Ochoński)

Map of German-occupied Europe in the Second World War: Ewa Możejko

Maps of Auschwitz I and Auschwitz II-Birkenau: Tadeusz Kinowski

Unaccredited photographs: All photographs of objects in the collections of the Auschwitz–Birkenau State Museum were taken by members of the Museum staff, notably Lidia Foryciarz, Zofia Łoboda, and Józefa Mostowik.

Other English-language Publications of the Auschwitz–Birkenau State Museum

Amidst a Nightmare of Crime: Manuscripts Found in Auschwitz of Prisoners in the Sonderkommando (1973).

Auschwitz: Death Camp. Monograph (in preparation).

Auschwitz: Voices from the Ground (1992). Photographic album.

Bibliography of KL Auschwitz, 1942–1980 (1991).

Halina Birenbaum, *Hope is the Last to Die* (1993).

Hope and Suffering: Artistic Creations of Auschwitz Prisoners (1989). Photographic album.

KL Auschwitz Seen by the SS: Rudolf Höss, Pery Broad, Johann Paul Kremer (1991).

Memorial Book. The Gypsies at Auschwitz–Birkenau (1993 in Association with KG Saur Verlag).

The Auschwitz–Birkenau State Museum also produces a wide range of publications in Polish, German, French, and Italian, including *Hefte von Auschwitz,* which is an Occasional Papers series appearing in German and Polish and containing historical studies. Enquiries regarding publications should be addressed to the Publications Department, Auschwitz–Birkenau State Museum, ul. Więźniów Oświęcimia 20, 32-603 Oświęcim 5, Poland.